The Way Home

The Way Home

How a Naive Single Mom Built her House in the Forest

Terry Faubert

STELLER BOOKS
Powell River

This story is true and the characters are real, to the best of the author's memory. Some details have been changed. All of the mistakes rest solely with the author.

*Dedicated to all the wonderful friends and neighbours
who helped my dreams become reality*

Table of Contents

"Whatever you can do or dream you can, begin it.
Boldness has genius, power and magic in it."

Goethe, *Faust, Part One,*
(as translated by John Anster)

Terry Faubert

Prologue

Who can predict those pivotal moments in our lives, when a path forks suddenly and irrevocably? For me, such a moment came early in 1983. It began at my friend Cristel's kitchen table. The happy sounds of our little boys' play warmed my soul as the tea-filled mug warmed my hands. Cristel was serious, calm, and sympathetic, the perfect friend to share my ideas with— however that day her words ruined my carefully crafted plans.

"That's not going to happen. You will never find someone like that here."

With these words I understood that I would have to rethink everything.

"Here" was Victoria, on the southern tip of Vancouver Island. For three years my son Jody and I had rented a cozy house bordering a playground. I made ends meet by looking after children, including Cristel's son, Tim, who was the same age as Jody and one of his best friends. Along with money for our groceries, childcare brought children into our home to be play companions for my only child. It had been wonderful, but something was shifting, the path beneath my feet rearranging itself. Rising rents had forced us to move every few years and my heart sank at the thought of Jody growing up without the continuity of a stable family home. Five years old, he was just starting to move from the cushioning safety of the home to the wider community. I realized it one day when he rode his little yellow tricycle down to the corner to mail a letter all by himself. I stood on the sidewalk outside our house and watched him. He was tiny for his age and pencil thin. His blond hair was just starting to darken, with the baby curls still turning up the long strands by his shoulders. Jody was bright-eyed and fresh-faced, with soft features, so cute his smile twisted the heartstrings of all who saw him. There was something symbolic about that small journey of independence. Up until now, it barely mattered for him where we lived, as long as I was there. But as he grew more and more self-reliant, his surroundings would affect what he learned and who he became.

Our house in Victoria

Jody on his tricycle

I was a big city girl, small and skinny, with wild curly hair and big brown eyes, born and raised in Toronto. I had attended university in Montreal, in love with the vibrant richness of life in a major cosmopolitan area. I had travelled to New York, Los Angeles, and Mexico City, energized by the mosaic of choices they offered. In my early twenties, I had vowed to only ever live in large cities, the larger the better. Moving to Vancouver, I had worried it might be too small for my liking, and assumed my time on the West Coast would be limited to a year or two.

But deep within the core of my being, something had changed. I realized that, although I lived in the city, I left it every chance I could. My son and I camped and hiked, picnicked and swam. There were birds to watch and squirrels to feed, parks and wilderness areas to explore. Near Port Renfrew on southern Vancouver Island at the edge of the San Juan River, black with tadpoles, I dreamed of camping forever while Jody followed toads and inspected newts. Nature made my heart sing, reminded me that my most precious memories came not from the flashing neon signs of downtown, but from the quiet Ontario lakes and valleys of the summer cottages of my

13

childhood. Did I want my son to grow up streetwise, or wise to the ways of nature? The choice was obvious. The way to get there was not.

At the San Juan River

My hope—my plan—was to meet someone who also felt this way. With no one to share the joyous milestones or the worrying uncertainties of raising a child, I often felt overwhelmed and bereft. And just plain lonely. At the same time, my experience of participating in the wondrous growth of this delightful child had been captivating and enjoyable beyond anything I had previously done. Still, Jody and I felt like half a family. I realized with a start one day that I wanted more children, and a loving partner to help care for them. Together we would move to the country and raise our family. However, no such man had yet materialized. It was easy enough to find dates in the city, but not any with men who embraced my dreams.

I shared my quest and my frustrations with Cristel that January day, and her reply startled me, her words carrying the force of truth.

"You won't find someone who wants to live in the

country here in Victoria. You have to move to the country to find guys like that."

That moment is frozen in time for me. Of course she was right; I saw it instantly. But ... move to the country all by myself, with a young child in tow? Was that even possible? I had done a number of brash, naive things in my life, but now I was pointed towards the craziest venture I would ever undertake.

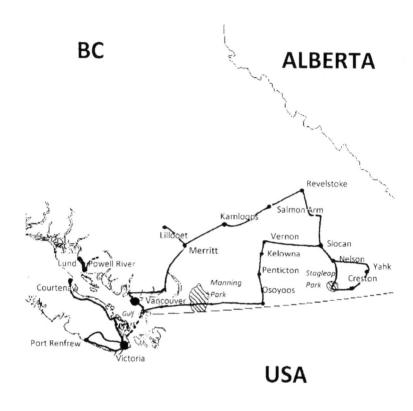

1. Searching All the Nooks and Crannies

In the midst of the bustle and noise of the Courtenay Art Fair, held on Vancouver Island, I sat painting the children's climbing structure, enjoying a quiet moment of reflection. My five-year-old son, Jody, played with the other children close by. It was July 1983 and we had been on the road for almost two months.

Spring had passed in a whirlwind of activity: the first step in my plan of action had been to buy a camperized van that we would live in while travelling the province in search of a small acreage. I knew very little about how to identify a good vehicle and was leery about being taken advantage of by unscrupulous sellers. Luckily I was part of the BCAA (British Columbia Automobile Association), which offered its members a $50 mobile car inspection. Since I was looking at lower-priced vans, it wasn't easy to find one that could pass inspection.

After several rejected vehicles, I had found a cute red van with a yellow stripe down the length of its body, at a Victoria dealership. The salesman tried hard to talk me out of paying for an inspection. He insisted their mechanic had already done one and handed me his glowing report. I admit I had wavered. The $50 fees were adding up with nothing to show for them but a sorry list of failed inspections. However, I held firm. The same friendly fellow came from BCAA for all of my inspections, and I was getting to know him. The cute van was a disaster, with major rust that had been hidden by the flashy paint and an engine showing signs of imminent failure. I was shocked at the salesman's bare-faced lies and vowed to avoid dealerships from then on.

Next I found a lovely yellow van with a large side bubble window. I was excited, but the seller refused to take my offered deposit, insisting it wasn't necessary. I was devastated when he sold it to a friend of his the day before my scheduled inspection. I was beginning to despair of ever achieving step one of my plan, when I came across a white 1969 Ford Econoline window van. It was the only one I had considered that I couldn't stand up in.

My affable inspector reported with a huge grin, "I think we've found you a van!"

Once the registration papers were signed, I could sell my current little car. Then, because I didn't have enough money to travel for the summer and pay rent too, I needed to sublet my sweet little house in Victoria. I only received one reply to my ad searching for a suitable tenant. The family seemed ideal apart from one glaring problem. They had a very large black dog. When I had first rented this house, the landlord had been adamant about no dogs. Cats weren't a problem, but Mr. Bauer, who worked during the week in his upholstery shop out back, made it absolutely clear that he would accept no dog in his rental. When I spoke to the eager family about it, they were still hopeful.

"He's a very old and quiet dog who won't do anything but sleep in the backyard."

Did I dare ask Mr. Bauer? He had always been so friendly during the two years we had lived in his cute little house, and seemed especially fond of Jody, who delivered his mail every day.

It was with much trepidation that I finally broached the subject with him, knocking bravely on the door to his workshop. To my immense surprise, he waved away all concerns, readily accepting the presence of lazy Oscar basking in the sun or lying in the shade. I hoped he was truly as barkless as they said!

Finally, with Jody, our tabby cat Furry, and her first litter of kittens, barely three weeks old, we set off around British Columbia to find some country land I could purchase with my meagre savings of $1,000. I hoped that would be enough for a down payment.

I knew I hadn't any chance of being able to afford a house. If I could purchase some land, I intended to return to Victoria for another year to earn enough to pay it off. I had heard too many stories of back-to-the-landers losing their property, unable to find work out in the country to make their payments. I was determined to pay off the land before moving onto it. In the absence of a house, I figured we could live on our hoped-for acreage in the van. I'd worry later about how to come up with a more permanent structure. Three to five acres of land sounded about right, and my hope was to find it far away from any town. I had a few leads—properties to look at—and the addresses of friends of friends to stay with, most of whom had been told to expect me. I also decided to place an ad in the magazine *Growing Without Schooling*, which was a constant source of inspiration and information as I homeschooled Jody. It read:

"Single mom with 5-year-old son and cat hoping for a place in the country in Canada. If you have one to share, rent, or sell, please let me know."

No one responded to the ad, but the magazine was still a help in my search because it included a directory of homeschooling families. There were some scattered across BC: in Kamloops, Nelson, Lumby, Duncan, Parksville, and Gibsons. I noted their addresses and planned our trip, based in part on where there might be like-minded people I could look up.

The passenger seat in the van turned backwards to face a fold-down table, which gave Jody a place to colour, do his puzzles, or play his games. I purchased and wrapped little toys and travel activities for him; every few days he would get something new to keep him interested and busy during the long hours of driving. Both he and Furry appreciated our frequent stops and a chance to get out and stretch our legs.

It was mid-May when we loaded up the white van in Victoria with all we would need for months on the road. Curtains graced all the windows and I made a matching curtained partition to block off the windshield for sleeping privacy. The tiny kittens were in a cardboard box across from the kitty litter bin, both tucked under the bed that stretched across the rear of the van. It was an exciting moment when I fired up the engine. It boggled my mind when the van reversed perfectly, then refused to go forward. Long trips can run into unforeseen complications, but we weren't even out of our parking area beside the house! What could be wrong? I had no idea. Sweat trickled down into my eyes, and Jody looked at me wonderingly. Reverse—no problem; forward—the van wouldn't budge an inch. And yet, previously, it had driven without difficulty. Surely something serious hadn't broken overnight? My frustration mounted. Would I have to unbuckle Jody and take the cats back into the house? It must have taken me twenty minutes of restarting the car, wiggling the gear shift, revving the engine, even peeking forlornly under the hood—before I finally noticed the parking brake was on! Then, to my great relief, the van drove forward smoothly. Blushing furiously, I belatedly set off, Jody and I cheering as we turned onto the street. I hoped such an inauspicious beginning didn't forewarn of a trip marred by stupid mistakes. Instead, I optimistically predicted I had gotten the hitches over and resolved at the very start, leaving only carefree days ahead.

We were headed first for Port Renfrew and our favourite camping spot on the San Juan River, near Lizard Lake—a misnomer since the lake teemed with newts, not lizards. This was our trial run through familiar territory before striking out into unknown parts of British Columbia. Even so, it turned into quite an adventure. The map showed a back roads return route through a place called Leechtown. Since I was bent on exploring and searching for land in all the obscure nooks and crannies of B.C., I bravely turned down the gravel road and drove for many hours without seeing a signpost or another car. When a pickup thundered towards us, I waved him down with great relief to ask directions. That's when I found out I would have to drive through a river to continue on this route.

When I finally reached the solitary house, sagging and derelict, that constituted Leechtown, the sight of a number of unsavoury-looking toughs drinking beer on the porch chilled me. They stared at my van, lurching to their feet. I didn't want to stop. The road ended at the river, and I couldn't see where it came out on the other side. Ignoring all risk, I drove into the fast-flowing water and across to where I could then see, just slightly down river, the road continuing on. My hands were shaking on the steering wheel, but I was laughing. I felt ready for anything after that.

On May 29, we headed for the Okanagan and the Kootenays, sleeping in our van, planning to give away the kittens as we went. We stayed with back-to-the-landers, homeschoolers, and free-thinkers. Other times we just parked somewhere on the side of the road, in which case finding a washroom was often a challenge, especially late at night and first thing in the morning. In Penticton, we were rudely evicted from a gas station washroom where we had gone to brush our teeth.

We chased down parcels of land everywhere. Most were too large and too expensive. Occasionally, without the slightest idea of what was involved, I suggested the owners subdivide. No one was interested.

High on a hill overlooking Osoyoos, in the midst of a community of teepees and other assorted strange structures, we checked out five acres that a bank had repossessed, The land itself, dry and desert-like, was owned communally; the five acres were really only a share in the acreage, not a separate, defined tract. This community was seeping with tensions, drugs, and crying, neglected children. One family had named their newborn Dove. In spite of her peaceful name, she was left all night in a tent by herself, where she couldn't be heard, so as not to interrupt her parents' sleep. It chilled me to think of her crying and defenceless in the dark wilderness, and I was shocked that her parents would speak to a stranger so flippantly about such a heartless practice. I was happy to turn my back on that piece.

I looked at a parcel of land just past Creston, where elk walked in the forest and government workers sparred with beavers that persevered in rebuilding the dam the employees continually kicked apart. Sadly, I had to reject that property too because it was situated between two roaring highways.

Snippets of scenes from this trip remain with me: my son on top of a high ridge in Manning Park, feeding ground squirrels, Jody perched on the head of an Ogopogo statue in Kelowna, and both of us posing with new friends in Vernon. Once we awoke, having parked overnight down a lonely country road, to find our van surrounded by cows! Another time, after a break at a roadside rest stop, I put Furry back in the van and drove thirty kilometres before realising she had jumped out an open window. With tears in my eyes, I headed back to the rest stop. Before we got there, we saw our dear little tabby cat running at top speed

along the side of the road in the direction we had gone. What a joyful reunion that was!

We made a good connection with a farm family in the Slocan Valley. Bonnie had a daughter Jessie, with an infectious smile and laughing eyes, who was the same age as Jody. She also had a curly-haired toddler, Rosie, and a goofy, troublesome poodle. We stopped there several times on our trip, the barefoot children playing happily while I helped on the farm to earn my keep.

At Stagleap Park high in the Selkirk Mountains, we marvelled at finding a half-frozen lake in June. We toured a house made of glass bottles at Boswell and spent most of a day at the Okanagan Game Farm. Jody lost his first tooth in Princeton.

missing tooth in Penticton

In Nelson, we stayed with Donna, a friend of Cristel's. My dear friend had also given us the phone number of her ex-husband. Helmut lived somewhere just outside Nelson. Jody's friend Tim would be spending the summer with his father and we were looking forward to possibly meeting up with him there. As soon as we were settled, I asked Donna if I could use her phone to call Helmut and Tim, but she shocked me by refusing.

"Oh, you don't want to visit him; he's horrible!"

She proceeded to regale me with tales of negative things Helmut had said and done, and she firmly insisted that we shouldn't contact him. My heart sank. We had promised Cristel and Jody had been looking forward to seeing Tim again. Sadly, I acquiesced. Donna wanted to take two of Furry's kittens. Because it was not quite the middle of June, they were still too young to leave Furry's side, so I made plans to pass through Nelson again in a week or so. I hoped to have another shot then at visiting Tim.

When we returned to Nelson, we met the same brick wall. Donna refused to let us phone Helmut or to tell us how to find his place. Once when I was driving with Donna in her car, she pointed him out as he walked down the sidewalk. I wanted to jump from the car right then. I think I would have if only Tim had been with him. It was true he looked somewhat solemn and unfriendly. I hesitated, and missed my chance. I was sad to leave Nelson with my promise unfulfilled.

Later, when I returned to Victoria, Cristel told me Tim had waited for us all summer, refusing to leave the house in case he might miss us. This tore my heart. When I explained what had happened, Cristel wasn't surprised. She knew Donna hated Helmut and would have tried to block us from contacting him. I so wished I had been more insistent and had followed my heart. And why had Cristel not warned us beforehand?

Tim's first words to Jody were, "Why did you never come?"

After Nelson, we continued east. In teeming rain, we knocked on doors on the outskirts of Yahk trying to find Kurt, another friend of Cristel's, but no one seemed to know him. As I knocked on another door, I realized the locked padlock meant no one could be home. Then around the corner came Kurt himself, soaked to the skin. I could have kissed him, I was so relieved! He welcomed us enthusiastically. When the rain stopped, he showed us around. I was intrigued by his approach to gardening: he built up raised beds with branches, then thinner ones, and finally twigs, followed by leaves and then grasses. Soil topped it all and the layers slowly composted, feeding the plants while maintaining the structure of the bed. Kurt extolled its virtues to me, explaining it was an old European method, known as "hugelkultur." I had never heard of such a wonderful garden. I stored away this brilliant idea, vowing to myself to make one just like it when I had my own place. I looked around Yahk for land for sale. There was actually a property available next to his, but it was flat and exposed. Having been logged, it was now a thin forest of young trees. I might have been able to purchase this piece, but it wasn't good enough to stop me looking elsewhere. Maybe I would be back if I didn't find anything better.

Upper Arrow Lake

From Yahk we headed north and took the Shelter Bay

Ferry across Upper Arrow Lake. It was so gorgeous there, my spirit soared, but when we tried to sleep in our van, rowdies came. They terrified us with their loud music and raucous voices, squealing their tires doing wheelies around the parking lot where we'd stopped for the night.

From there we went through Revelstoke where gas was so expensive at thirty-four cents a litre that I refused to buy any and risked going on in spite of the gas gauge hovering near empty. On through Sicamous and Salmon Arm to Kamloops and its lovely Riverside Park. We finally ended up in Merritt, where we heard of a "Survival Gathering," a wilderness meet-up of like-minded people sharing stories, discussions, and music to "save the earth." It would take place up by Lillooet towards the end of July. But before that, we had to go back to Vancouver Island.

My friend Bob had a job working in the daycare at the Courtenay Art Fair, known today as the Filberg Festival. He managed to get me a job there too, and I welcomed the chance to earn a bit of money during my trip, as well as check out a new area. Arriving back on the coast, I was struck by how much I had missed the beauty of the ocean and the mountains. How could I think of moving to the Interior?

I mused on these recent travels while I continued to paint the children's climbing structure at the Fair. Perhaps I should go north, maybe try up in the Queen Charlotte Islands. It was then that Sandy walked into the daycare with her delightful young daughter Willow. They made a contrasting sight, Sandy with her short dark hair holding Willow's hand, whose long blond hair spilled down her back. Sandy had an announcement. There was to be a "Healing Gathering" up Powell Lake at the beginning of August. They needed people to work in the day care there. Were any of us interested?

"I'll go," I said, without a moment's hesitation, though I had no idea where Powell Lake was.

In fact, it turned out that it wasn't even on Vancouver Island! Powell Lake stretches north and east of the town of Powell River, where Sandy and Willow lived. It is on the mainland at the top of the Sunshine Coast, a ferry ride across from Vancouver Island and two ferries up from the city of Vancouver.

That adventure was still weeks ahead. First, after finding a home for the last kitten at the Fair, we headed back to Lillooet and somehow found the way up a maze of back roads to the Survival Gathering held in the middle of nowhere. Our days were filled with songs, music, shared food, discussions, and tales around the bonfire before we once again hit the road. From there we returned to the coast and island-hopped through the Gulf Islands. And that's when Furry decided she'd had enough of the roving life. Up until then, we had let her out whenever we stopped, calling her back when it was time to go. Now she seemed to grow more and more reluctant to return. Finally, she surprised us by suddenly turning and disappearing into the bushes when we called. We had a ferry to catch and we couldn't find her. I began to despair of ever seeing her again. How long could we wait? It took us forty minutes, but we finally got her, and coincidentally, the ferry was forty minutes late, pulling in just as we drove up. After that, Furry's roaming days were over. From then on she could only go outside with a harness and leash.

The Powell Lake Healing Gathering was held far out in the wilderness on Peter and Linda's land, which would later become Fiddlehead Farm. On arriving in Powell River, I met up with Sandy and learned to my dismay that the farm was only accessible by boats, which had been pre-arranged to take all the participants. What about Furry? There was no way I could imagine clutching a squirming terrified cat on a loud boat crammed with strangers. Even if I tried to transport her in a box, she would be sure to run off in panic upon its opening, especially in the uncertain confines of a shared tent. I told Sandy I wouldn't be able to come after all, but she had a solution. During the gathering, her cat would be looked after in her Powell River house; why didn't I just leave Furry there? I hesitated, but in the end she convinced me. And so, after a hurried goodbye to our dainty tabby cat who had accompanied us to so many places, we stood with a group of people waiting for a boat at the marina near the bridge where Powell Lake meets the short river that gave the town its name.

Jody was impatient, shading his eyes from the brightness and asking countless times, "When will the boat come?"

It was a beautiful August day, the sun smiling down on us and the tiniest of breezes teasing the waves across the large expanse of deep blue water. When the boat finally appeared, I was shocked to see an open aluminum skiff. Everyone climbed in and we pushed off, motoring on and on, forty minutes and more. The land around us became increasingly rugged and, after passing a few isolated float homes, all signs of people dropped away. There was much chatter aboard, and many questions as to who we were and how we came to be there. Some broke into song. Most of the women removed their shirts and I was happy to join them, feeling free and comfortable, and safely out of sight of prying eyes. Apparently not though. I thought it both hilarious and shocking when I later heard that some people in the float homes we passed thought the farm was a nudist colony.

At last the sound of the motor slowed and we pulled in to a dock, but the journey was not over yet. It was another half hour or more to walk from the water's edge up to our destination. We followed along narrow trails fringed by tall trees and dense bushes that opened at last to sunny fields. In spite of the presence of many people, the farm was peaceful and serene, its animals contented, and its common buildings welcoming. Jody spent so much time running and playing naked in the sunshine, his little rear became sunburned. I met wonderful people, beginning friendships that would last for years. Most participants lived in or had previously lived in the area around Powell River and Lund, though some came from much further afield.

Peter and Linda's Farm

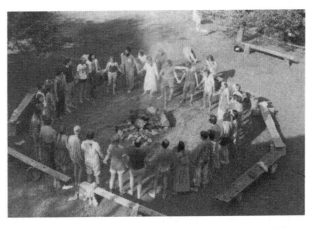

A small group dressed all in red or purple held their own separate rituals, as well as joining in the general activities. These individuals were followers of a guru named

Rajneesh. They had given up their own names in favour of a "sannyasin" name bestowed on each by the guru. To my great surprise, an old friend from Montreal, who I hadn't seen for seven years, was one of them! I couldn't stop calling him by his old name of John, much to his annoyance. I enjoyed talking with a French Canadian member of this cult whose sannyasin name was "Prem" and we partnered up for a few of the activities. Though most of my time was spent in a fenced-off area looking after the children, I did attend some of the workshops, held out in the open fields by day and around the campfires in the dark.

The night skies were a canopy of brilliant stars, the Milky Way splashing through them. Once, long after midnight, with Jody fast asleep in our shared tent, I was awed by the white streaks of northern lights blazing across the sky.

As the five days passed, I noticed a large bulletin board where people posted notices of activities or of rides needed. I was struck by an idea and quickly penned my own notice: "Looking for Land." Three different people sought me out—all telling me about the same piece of land, up Baggi Road in Lund. The term "Lund" roughly defined a large forested area north of Powell River that included, but wasn't limited to, the actual village of Lund. A man called Peter was selling six and a quarter acres of a tenancy in common land. This meant that his parcel was part of an undivided forty-five acres, which were shared with four other couples. Legally, each held only a share of the entire piece, but these members had agreed to mark off individual portions to call their own. A new person wishing to purchase part of this tenancy in common had to sign a document agreeing to a dozen terms, including a prohibition on clear-cut logging—which all sounded fine to me.

A guy named Jeffrey suggested Jody and I join others staying on after the Gathering at his place on Craig Farm so that we could check it out. When he gave me a tour of his beautiful, funky house, one feature stood out. Jeffrey was proud of his "wood door." In the wall by the wood stove, down near the floor, was a little door that could be opened to bring in pieces of firewood from an attached outside storage area. How clever! No mess of firewood stacked inside. No need to bundle up and go out in the cold to fetch more when the fire needed stoking. I was impressed. I'd never seen such a feature before. I decided then and there to include it in my hoped-for house.

2. The Best Green

Not knowing what to expect, Jody and I headed up the two-lane, winding highway north from Craig Road to the tiny village of Lund. Half an hour and more north of Powell River, Lund was, and still is, a sleepy little village, where Highway 101 ends with a hill straight down to the wharf. Its few streets of houses look out to gorgeous sunsets amid picturesque islands of tall trees and rocky cliffs. The large hotel that dominates the village includes a post office and an old-fashioned general store, crowded with both necessities and frivolities. Water taxis drone to and from Savary Island's white sands, and both fishing and cruising boats crowd its marina.

In 1983, there was a Community Centre, a large building covered in dark brown siding near the top of the hill, and a gas station at the corner where we turned north of the village onto Finn Bay Road. We kept going, each turn bringing us deeper into the bush until the forest crowded the road. When we set off to explore on foot, we found the land for sale was thick with trees, so thick we had to push our way through. "Second growth," the neighbours said. Boughs creaked and groaned in the wind. Branches and cones littered the ground, scattered among the rocks. Salal towered over Jody's head and obscured the uneven footing. There was a silence broken only by the occasional call of an unseen bird. Jody, whose favourite colour was green, proclaimed it "the best green I ever saw."

Peter had never lived on this piece, though he had stayed nearby in a cabin with his partner Caryl. He had, however, created a large garden on this parcel before selling half of the land to Jeff and Darcie. Now he was hoping to sell the rest—a six and a quarter acre piece. Jeff was very welcoming, and though I later learned he could be impatient, he was always ready to help. I had no idea that day how much I would come to rely on this smiling, bearded neighbour and his kind-hearted, fair-haired wife, Darcie. Jeff showed me around, leaving Jody to play with his two daughters. Terra, who was almost exactly Jody's age, was friendly and full of life. Her little sister, Shanti, was shy and sweet, hiding her face when I spoke to her. Jeff took me to meet the other members of the tenancy in common who lived there: Neil and Linda, Jack and Audrey. The remaining couple, Martin and Janet, lived in town. Everyone was friendly and helpful, with interesting and unique houses, at varying levels of completion. They lived in them while transitioning through many construction stages: Jeff and Darcie's bathtub stood brashly in their living room; Neil and Linda's family of four were squeezed into a tiny geodesic dome covered in hand-cut cedar shakes.

I truly had little money to purchase property. The $1,000 down payment I had scrimped and saved for so long to put aside, and the $10,000 offer I was determined to hold to, both seemed embarrassingly small. Peter was asking $18,000.

The neighbours were encouraging. "He's been trying to sell for years. He really needs the money now, to build an addition to his house. There's no one else interested. Make him an offer."

This was by far the best piece of land I had seen in almost three months of travelling. I was pretty sure it was out of my reach.

Peter was a small fellow with a big heart and a kind smile. When I sat at his kitchen table, I could see the hope in his eyes.

"So, what do you think? Do you want to buy it?"

I kept my shaking hands under the table. "That's way too much money." I watched his spirits drop as I tremulously outlined my terms: $10,000 with $1,000 down.

Silence. Then: "How about $16,000? I started out at 28."

I shook my head miserably. "I can't go higher than $10,000."

He stared at me thoughtfully. "Let me think about it," he said. "I'll see what I can come up with."

I didn't have much hope, but the next time we met, there was a determined gleam in his eye. He would reduce the price to $12,000 if I could come up with a down payment of $8,000 by October first, and would agree to pay $2,000 per year for the next two years without interest.

I tried to insist on the ten, but he wouldn't budge. In the end I agreed, and paid him a $1,000 deposit in hundred dollar bills, more cash than I had ever held before in my trembling hands. We both stared at the money, giggling at how silly it was that slim pieces of paper could be worth so much. They felt so fragile.

"We could just burn them," Peter joked, his dark eyes twinkling.

I knew what he was feeling. I left them carelessly stacked on his kitchen table and hurried back to Victoria to search out the missing $7,000. I had not let on how hopeless that seemed. Where could I ever find that much money so quickly?

The people who had sublet my rented house in Victoria were willing to stay on through September, so at least I would not have to pay rent that month. I couldn't face living four more weeks in the confining space of our low-ceilinged van, so we stayed at the house of two delightful little girls, Magdalene and Philippa, who I babysat: free child minding in exchange for housing. Other children were dropped off, giving me some income. Unfortunately, all did not go smoothly. Greg and his wife hadn't expected so many children running around their yard. They certainly didn't want such a crowd in their house if it rained! I too hadn't thought so many of my former charges would all show up at the same time. It seemed the families had missed us during our travels and were all eager to take up my babysitting service once again. I definitely didn't want to turn any away, given my tenuous financial situation. So I put out the call to my network of families. Would anyone trade housing for babysitting for the rest of September? Luckily, the answer was yes.

Jody turned six on the twenty-first of September, a beautiful sunny day, cool in the morning but quite warm by afternoon. We were staying upstairs at Penny's house. I had babysat her two boys for years and was grateful for her letting us stay there. Her older boy Christopher, probably about eight then, was like an older brother to Jody. I was determined to put aside my cares and worries about the money and the land, and make Jody's birthday a happy occasion.

And so it was. I arranged Jody's presents beside his bed and he opened them before going down to breakfast. He was thrilled with them all and wanted to set up the Playmobil Gas Station then and there. Afterward, we biked down to the Land of the Little People in Heritage Village. Jody was especially delighted with the train that ran when he pushed a button. We spent some time getting it to stop just right in the sun for a photo. We followed this with shrimp soup and a Hawaiian dessert at our favourite restaurant, Goodies.

Back at Penny's house, I scrambled Jody into his party clothes before his young friends began to arrive. Each of the six guests joined the table to work with scissors, crayons, pipe cleaners, and play dough. Active games followed: Doggie, Doggie, Who's Got Your Bone?, Hot Potato, Giant Step. Birthday cake was next—coconut butter with honey butter icing decorated with strawberries. Surprise! I had baked the cake with coins hidden inside it, wrapped in wax paper.

After eating, the children fished for prizes, catching the wrapped packages on hooks made from coat hangers that dangled from makeshift fishing rods. Then we all walked down to the library. Each child chose one book to take home and I read aloud to them the birthday boy's choice. The party over, Jody spent much of the evening playing with his new toys. It was always our tradition to allow Jody to stay up on his birthday till his actual time of birth, 8:45 pm, so that was when he was tucked contentedly into bed with his new stuffed penguin beside him.

Would this be his last birthday in Victoria? Only if I could somehow come up with the money to meet Peter's terms. I spent my free time going from bank to bank, but none would consider loaning me $7,000; a good credit rating does not make up for a paltry income.

One crisp autumn morning a few days after Jody's birthday, he was invited to play with his friend Tim. It was Tim's mom, Cristel, whose advice had sent me off searching for land. We sat around her kitchen table once again, watching the boys play. They were like two bookends, both cute, bright, and soft-featured, innocently laughing. I miserably told Cristel of the piece of land I was trying to buy and how I had exhausted all possibilities for a loan.

"I can loan you that much," she stated blandly.

I could only stare. Cristel? A single mom who barely seemed to have enough to get by? Surely she was joking.

But she was not. Unbelievably, she had money in a term deposit and was willing to lend it to me at the same interest rate it was currently earning, if I would pay it all back within a year. I wasn't sure how I could do that, but I was willing to just take it one step at a time.

Jody and Tim

So, defying all odds, thanks to Cristel's generosity I came up with the rest of the down payment just before the deadline. When I tried to call Peter with the good news, I ran into an unexpected snag. In the Powell River area, I had been surprised to discover that only five digits were needed to make a local telephone call. From Victoria, the area code plus seven digits were necessary. It was easy enough to find the area code, but not the two numbers I was still missing. The operator was perplexed when I asked for assistance, unable at first to believe there was anywhere in BC that continued to only require five numbers be dialed. When she finally understood and told me it would be "4, 8," I was able to delight Peter with the success of my financing. Using Peter's instructions, I had a lawyer, against his better judgement, draw up a promissory note for the remainder, with no interest and no penalty or recourse for non-payment.

When September ended and my subtenants moved out, I

was relieved to be living once again in my rented house. Now I had to make money, lots of money, in the hope of moving debt-free onto our land by next summer. I applied for and obtained a whole number of part-time jobs in Victoria, which I was able to fit in around each other, sometimes over-lapping them so I was paid for more than one at the same time. Babysitting was easy: the more children I took in, the higher my hourly wage. Jody delighted in having more and more friends coming over to play. I also managed to get an overnight position, sleeping at the house of a single father who was an all-night janitor. In the morning I would get his four young children, and Jody, up, dressed, and fed. The six-year-old would stay to be picked up for school, but I was responsible for dropping the two-year-old at her aunt's and the four-year-old twins at a daycare on our way home. It was a rush, but we would usually get home about ten minutes before the first child arrived at my house for babysitting. When I had to pick up a child from school, I would pile everyone into the van.

As well, I worked at a child-minding service in a Recreation Centre. I would bring the children I was babysitting to this drop-in, hugely increasing my wage for that hour or two. Often the children I brought along free out-numbered the paid ones. Occasionally, no one else used the service and those freebies were the only ones there.

On top of all those positions, I taught after school courses at a couple of recreation centres, the only jobs where Jody couldn't come along. Six years old now, homeschooled and an avid reader, Jody would hang out alone at the public library during these courses. A pile of books beside him, he became the favourite of the children's librarian, who regaled me with tales of his astute questions and charming interests.

In this way I worked around the clock and squirreled away almost all I earned, retaining the bare minimum we needed to live on. When December rolled around, there wasn't any extra for Christmas. With a week remaining before the big holiday, I had only ten dollars left to spend and no food but a bag of potatoes. Jody wanted a Christmas tree. It was a hard decision, but I bought the ten dollar tree and we ate potatoes for three days. After that a donated Christmas hamper arrived; it was like a miracle: two shopping carts full of food and a twenty-pound turkey besides. There were even mandarin oranges and crackers, which we ate in bed Christmas morning, and a pumpkin pie for dessert after our supper feast. The volunteers distributing the hampers had no idea what it meant to us. It was all I could do to hold back my tears when they arrived.

Jody surprised me by stuffing my stocking with little gifts he made in secret. He cut out little pictures from old Christmas cards, some of which stood up with bases he made for them. There were also small games he invented, a beautiful Santa Claus picture he drew, dough ornaments he had painted, and a wool Santa, all fashioned by his clever young fingers. As if that wasn't enough, he bought me an adorable little glass container at the Children's Christmas Store, which excluded anyone over twelve years old and featured gifts for a few dollars each.

I bought him a toy train and asked my parents to pay for his first two-wheel bike. Under the tree, after unwrapping the train, which thrilled him, he found a note. He was able to read it easily by himself, and follow its directions to the green bike which stood waiting enticingly on its training wheels, plastic rainbow streamers brightening the ends of the handlebars. Jody went to bed happy that night. His only regret was not yet riding his new bike. I fell exhausted into bed, content that peace and joy had been spread so simply.

At one of the Victoria craft fairs we visited that Christmas season, there was a calligraphy booth. For a donation, an artist would write your name in beautiful lettering. Jody had a different idea: he wanted the fellow to pen "The Best Green I Ever Saw," a phrase that had come to epitomize our newly-purchased land. That lovely sign would hang on Jody's wall for years to come.

Through that winter and spring, I worked every day, scrimping and cutting corners, watching my debt dwindling. It was in May that I got an unexpected phone call from Martin, a member of my Lund tenancy in common. He did not live on his land, but there was an old cabin there—the same cabin Peter once lived in and where Peter's son Towagh had been born. People were now staying uninvited in this cabin and leaving garbage all around. Martin had an offer for me: I could live in the cabin as long as I wanted, rent-free, if I would get rid of it when I left. He suggested I burn it down. I was delighted! We would have a place to live when we first arrived that would be so much better than the van or our tent. But I knew I would never burn it down. I needed a cabin to live in. Why didn't I move it onto my property instead!

3. The Good, the Bad, and the Awful

When the day of our long-awaited move finally arrived, we headed north in bright summer sunshine. It was the July holiday weekend 1984 and there was no time for backward glances. We were leaving our Victoria city life behind and setting out into the unknown.

At a garage sale, I had sold all my furniture and, since we would be living "off the grid," all the electrical devices that I could. Only the rocking chair that I refinished for Jody's birth and an unsold string of Christmas lights defied that edict. The garage sale profits added on to my final pay cheques were the only funds in my pocket.

I had often experienced living on next to nothing. When I was a child, my father worked in factories with low pay and the ever-present threat of lay-offs. "We can't afford it," was a constant refrain as I was growing up. A box of outgrown clothes dropped off from my older cousins held all the promise of a surprise parcel. Two of my mother's favourite sayings were: "A penny saved is a penny earned" and "Look after the pennies and the dollars will take care of themselves." As a child, I took this proffered wisdom to heart, pocketing the ten cents Mom gave me for school milk money each day and drinking water instead. On the one day a week I was to buy a hot lunch at the school cafeteria, I saved the money and bought only a glass of milk. When I was a starving student in Montreal, I scrimped by on the barest minimum, quickly realizing that, while rent and other bills were fixed, I was free to spend as much or as little as I wanted on food. The past year also, with over seventy-five percent of my earnings going to service my debts to Cristel and Peter, had seen me living well below the poverty line. I wasn't worried about my lack of money now; I was confident I could manage somehow, as I'd always done before.

Jody's dad, Duncan, with his long-time girlfriend, Monica, offered to help us move. My relationship with Duncan survived years of ups and downs, on and off, but through it all we remained friends. Now my white van and Duncan's bright orange one were crammed with boxes containing the necessary and the unsold. Squeezed in among them were Jody, our steadfast Furry, and one remaining kitten from her second litter. We found homes for her other two kittens, but not for the tabby-striped male, the only one that Jody had named. When these kitties first opened their eyes, this little guy peered out of only one, his other remaining shut for a few more days. Jody thought he looked like a one-eyed pirate and even after his second eye came unglued, we continued to call him Pirate. I thought it a happy coincidence that it was this kitten with a name who would remain part of our family.

The beauty of the drive and the peaceful glide of a summer ferry were lost on me. With a mix of exhilaration and trepidation, I looked toward our destination, scarcely able to believe it was really happening.

The road from Powell River to Lund, jokingly called a highway, was winding and picturesque, lined with a tangle of tall trees and impenetrable bushes. Once past the village, each turn brought a narrower, rougher road with large potholes filled with puddles of varying depths.

On the way there, Duncan and Monica had some big news for me. When we stopped to confer about directions, they shared with me their plan to marry in September, dashing my unconscious hopes for an eventual reconciliation. I strove to congratulate them in a normal voice, ignoring the sudden pounding of my heart. When I shakily climbed back into my van, I blurted out the news to Jody in such a way that he began to sob. Guilt was thrown into the mix of my confused emotions. I pulled over and left Duncan to reassure his son and to see how upsetting his news was—not to me, to Jody—but Duncan knew what was going on, that in fact, in spite of the seven years since the end of our relationship, I had never gotten over him or given up hope that we might get back together.

Part of me wished that he was marrying me; another part thought perhaps now at last I would be able to truly move on from wanting him to finding the partner I hoped for.

By the time we reached the tenancy in common land, bushes scraped the vans on either side. We bumped over two inlaid logs that spanned the road. They formed a channel, diverting water from one side to the other. At the top of a long, steep hill we found the old cabin.

We arrive!

The interior was littered with rat droppings, the outside with mattresses and other discarded junk. A ladder led up to a loft under the barn-shaped roof. A giant black ant guarded a hole in the flooring up there; stepping on him released a horde of his tribe and Jody took on the task of stomping on them all several times a day. A single layer of bare, uninsulated plywood formed the walls. A loose piece of plywood hid a gaping hole in the floor where the bottom of the tin woodstove had burnt through.

Before anything could be unloaded, the whole place had to be swept out. One of the first things unpacked were our special mugs, strategically placed where I could find them immediately. To commemorate this momentous move, I had purchased brand new mugs for myself and Jody. What made them even more significant was that I almost never bought anything that wasn't second-hand. Mine showed a graceful white goose in three-dimensional relief, a pastel blue and pink ribbon around its neck. It was by far the most gorgeous mug I have ever owned. Jody's was a brightly coloured scene of hot air balloons against a background of yellow mountains, sturdy and stable where mine was delicate and fragile. I lifted them carefully out of the first box and unwrapped them, placing them proudly on the wobbly handmade table that dominated the main floor of the tiny cabin.

A first drink to celebrate our arrival! I poured out the juice. Jody and I smiled at each other over the rims as I explained their significance to Duncan and Monica, who declined to join us. My beautiful mug would not survive our first year here, though my son still uses his more than thirty years later.

Jody at the Lookout

We quickly finished unloading Duncan's van, then all four of us hiked up to a nearby lookout with a gorgeous view of the ocean, the mountains, and Savary Island. My heart was filled with the beauty and peace of these surroundings and I felt ready to take on the challenges ahead.

When darkness fell, I carried little Pirate safely up the steeply slanted ladder to spend the night with us. It would only be a few days before he surprised us by climbing all the way up there by himself. That night Jody and I slept on a mattress on the loft floor, keeping Furry close as insurance against rats. In the dark I could hear her dispatching them and I gritted my teeth and closed my eyes tightly. What a relief to see the morning sunshine at last! Beneath me, I discovered a tail protruding from under my pillow where Furry had stashed the hind quarters of a rat. Yuck! While sweeping out the house yet again the next day, I noticed that the squashed ants had all mysteriously disappeared. In the days to come, as Jody continued his stomping ant patrol, I realized we were finally rid of them only when the dead ones remained ungathered.

Pirate on the mattress in the loft,
wearing a hat Jody made for him

Jeff and Darcie's girl, Terra, (or Rainbow, as she insisted we call her that day and for the next few months) came over to play and I set up Jody's play table outside for their breakfast and snacks. Their golden laughter rippled through the bright air. Jody was delighted and excited to have a whole new world to explore, and a friend to share it with. It seemed almost unbelievable that we were really here, after all the planning, all the hardships and deprivations, all the long hours of work in the city. Now we were off in the forest, away from all those pressures. I felt the rest of our lives would be like a vacation, a satisfying working vacation.

With hasty goodbyes and last minute hugs, Duncan and Monica drove away. We waved as their bright orange van disappeared down the hill and the noise of their engine dwindled to the peace and quiet of our new surroundings, punctuated by childish giggles. We were seemingly in the middle of nowhere. And we were on our own.

4. Wild and Free

The camperized van served us well, filling our little house with amenities. I removed its small propane stove and set it up inside to cook our food. One of the bench seats was pried loose and hauled up the ladder to the loft, a perfect little bed for Jody. The icebox became a food cupboard. I dug a pit by the front stairs and sank our metal Coleman cooler. The finish would be scratched and scraped, the hinges and catch would rust, but I was proud to have devised our own little root cellar, where perishables stayed cool in summer and wouldn't freeze in winter. A yellow plastic baby bath was where we washed, standing in the warmed water and sponging off the dust and dirt as best we could.

We fell easily into the rhythm of life in the forest. The long summer days blessed us, warming our hearts with wild flowers and bird songs. Eagles soared from the tops of the tallest trees; nighthawks dove thrumming after invisible insects. The teeniest tree frogs chirped unseen. Silent deer daintily stepped into view, freezing at the slightest sound. When startled, they bounced away in huge leaps, gone from sight in an instant, leaving only swinging branches to attest to their passage. We listened spellbound to owls call after dark and once I glimpsed a flying squirrel glide through moonlit branches.

Sleep seemed so much deeper and more refreshing in the absolute quiet and dark of the forest. I had been unaware how much traffic noise and city lights had bothered my nighttimes. With all the other urban sources of light, the moon had been a minor player, hardly noticeable. So I was greatly surprised at how the phases of the moon strongly affected our nights. In the dark of the moon, we couldn't see to take one step outside. A full moon gave a bright but soft illumination, lending a touch of magic to our surroundings, and casting definite shadows. In moonlight, we could walk outdoors without even needing a flashlight.

Bedtime for Jody had always included a story. I loved to read aloud, modulating my voice to enhance the words of the different characters. Now, in the hushed darkness of the cabin's loft, I sat on the edge of the mattress and each night read a chapter from *The Railway Children* by Edith Nesbit, while Jody listened with rapt attention. This book had been given to him as a going-away present from close friends in Victoria, with the inscription, "Best wishes for your new adventure." It was the first of many bedtime books I would read to him in Lund, from classics like *Robinson Crusoe* and *Black Beauty*, to Enid Blyton's adventures, and *The Little House on the Prairie* series. Reading him a bedtime story created a special bubble of focused time for the two of us, and a loving end to his day.

Each morning, we eagerly explored our new world, finding the paths that led up to views or down to hideaways. I checked out identification guides from the Powell River library and happily searched out the names of new birds and plants: towhee, junco, flicker; lupine, bog violet, monkey flower.

The small library was tucked into the basement of the City Hall. We were at first mystified, unable to find it. I finally walked up the steps and into the front door of the City Hall, but it didn't look promising.

I hesitatingly inquired, "Is there a library in here?"

The entrance was actually hidden around the rear of the building, and though tiny, the library was a repository of all the information I needed to successfully work through the intricacies of our new lifestyle. I envisioned a homestead that included chickens and goats; my wilder dreams saw us with a horse or honey bees. But one thing was without doubt: we would certainly need a dog first of all. I pored through books on different types of dogs, compiling stark lists of their pros and cons. Our best friend and companion should be good with children, intelligent and easily trained, protective and suited to life in the bush. Not overly large and definitely not too small. In the end, I narrowed the list to a few breeds, and ranked them. The perfect dog appeared to be a type I had never heard of: Belgian Sheepdog, a breed that would in later years be renamed Belgian Shepherd. It met all my requirements, plus I loved the beauty of its Tervuren variety, with a long, tawny-coloured coat and black face. I began sending out inquiries to breeders, none of whom lived in BC, hoping to line up a Belgian puppy as soon as the house was complete. Little did I know that within a year, a blond spaniel named Max would drop unchosen into our family or that one day, a decade later, an amazing Belgian Sheepdog would caper through our life and into our hearts forever.

One day a week became our designated town day. Of course there was always the mandatory stop at the library, for books, the use of a washroom, and often just a place to rest. The main library was the best for all of those, but our favourite library was in the old part of town, known as the Townsite. It was also hidden away, down some steps around the side of Dwight Hall, an imposing old building full of character and charm. This library was even smaller, but Jody loved it for its Tintin books, which were hard to get at the main branch, but here they always sat available and inviting on the shelves. There was a lovely fountain in the little park beside Dwight Hall and on warm days we would sit there to eat our lunch and read our books before making the long drive back to Lund and the old cabin.

We also discovered the outdoor pool near J.P. Dallas School. It was a busy pool, full of laughing, splashing children. However, it wasn't swimming in the sunshine and fresh air that attracted us, it was the showers. At this pool, people showered before paying to go in the water, so our much needed showers were free. Once summer ended, the outdoor pool closed, and our vital town day showers switched to the Recreation Complex. In the beginning, telling the receptionist we were only showering was also without charge. After a while though, the Complex began charging a small showering fee; eventually they required those showering to pay the same entrance fee as swimmers, explaining that they "couldn't be certain someone who said they were only showering wouldn't go in the pool." Sigh.

Powell River had a credit union, tucked away down a small alley in Townsite. I would need to make the first of the two remaining payments to Peter for my land come fall. Before leaving Victoria, I had managed to put away just enough money in two term deposits: given the current 10% rate of interest, the first would grow to the $2,000 I owed this fall and the second would swell to the final $2,000 just in time for the last payment. I was unaware that interest rates could vary or that this was a particularly high rate which would not always be available.

To my horror, Peter suddenly called in this debt. He and his wife had a new baby, and the addition for his small house on the beach just north of town was running over budget. He asked me if I could pay off all that I owed immediately. My heart thumping, I explained that I didn't actually have the money yet. If I cashed in the term deposits early, I would be short by hundreds of dollars.

53

Peter offered to waive the rest if I would pay now what I had. And so it was done. My meagre savings were depleted and I suddenly owned the land outright, free and clear.

At least once a week, we walked into the village of Lund, mainly to get the mail. We discovered the shortcuts: the more direct routes down trails and across neighbours' properties that would spit us out near the intersection of Baggi and Finn Bay Roads. Jody searched for pop cans along the roadsides and in the ditches, hoping to find enough to cash in for an ice cream bar at the Lund Store. He was usually successful.

Our mail came "General Delivery," which meant it was held for us behind the counter in the tiny post office squeezed between the hotel lobby and the general store. Saundra was the friendly postal worker behind the counter, and she always had a kind word for Jody and myself. It wasn't long before my volume of mail earned me the honour of a separate pigeonhole cubby for my letters. Our mailing address went up a notch, from simply "General Delivery, Lund" to "Box 89, General Delivery, Lund." I was inordinately proud to have achieved this small symbol of belonging.

It wasn't long after arriving that I received a disturbing letter. My friend, Cristel, who had been so instrumental in supporting this grand adventure and had loaned me the money for the down payment on this land, now demanded more interest. I was shocked. My loan from her had been paid off months prior, including all the interest I owed. Cristel's letter explained how loaning me those funds cost her a couple of hundred dollars. She had withdrawn the money from a term deposit, charging me the same interest rate it was paying. She had neglected to calculate that I only paid interest on what was still outstanding; each time I made a payment, my interest owing decreased, yet she could not immediately reinvest my payments for such a return.

I understood what she meant, but I was stuck. I did not have that much extra money, having just managed to squeak by paying what I owed to her and to Peter. My new friends were adamant—she could not charge interest on money once I had repaid it. I felt very bad about the whole situation, sad and even guilty that she was out some money, yet resentful that she would try at this late date to alter our agreed on terms to try to recoup what I couldn't deliver. I don't remember if I even answered her letter. Sadly, I never heard from her again. One of my closest friendships came to an abrupt end. Decades later, I discovered that Cristel returned soon after to her native Germany, leaving Tim to be raised by his father in Nelson. I was also surprised to discover that Tim grew up to become a well-known country singer based in Calgary.

Here in our new community, Jody and Terra quickly became fast friends. They were practically inseparable. Darcie cut a direct trail between her house and the old cabin and most days they chose randomly which house they would play at. One time, they were up in the old cabin's loft having fun on the bed, when Terra's foot pushed against a window and dislodged its pane of glass. I heard the crash and rushed out to see splinters everywhere and two frightened faces peeking out of the sudden opening. The wooden window frame was rotten, so it was not a big loss, just a hazardous mess to pick up. I found an old piece of screen to staple over the gap; cardboard would eventually block the light and the view of trees I had so enjoyed waking up to.

There didn't seem to be any reason why I would need a clock here. I wanted to live free of such ordered restrictions, in tune with nature and the rhythms of the forest. I put away my watch and attempted to feel my way naturally through each day. Then came the day that seemed to never end. I expected the sun to soon begin its descent, but strangely, the sky stayed bright blue. The day just went on and on. When I chanced to see my neighbour, Dan, I asked him what time it was and stared in bewilderment at his answer. It was only two o'clock in the afternoon, yet we had eaten supper many hours before! How was that possible? What time did we get up that morning? The clock-free experiment was over; I would never again go a day without wearing a watch.

Dan was my closest neighbour. He lived in a haphazardly-built little cabin beside a large pond. On the edge of this pond, just down the hill from the cabin where we lived, was an old-fashioned sauna, complete with a bed of stones that could be heated and a metal bucket to scoop pond water for pouring on these stones to generate steam. This was why the road that ran by our old cabin was known as Sauna Road. One of the first times we spoke to Dan, he warned us not to worry if we occasionally heard him yelling. After becoming super-heated in the sauna, he would jump directly into his shockingly chilly pond, vocalizing when his naked body hit the water. Indeed, we would sometimes be startled by a blood-curdling scream coming from that direction. Jody and I would stop what we were doing to stare at each other, then burst into laughter.

That summer, Jeff and Darcie offered us the use of a garden bed or two by their house. I was anxious to put Kurt's raised bed plan into action, but Jeff was less than thrilled with the idea of branches and twigs in his garden. He understood the reasoning behind it, but didn't want me to try such a different method in his established garden. Disappointed, I followed his instructions reluctantly, putting on hold my vision—next year, when I had my own garden!

Jody had always been homeschooled, in the tradition of John Holt's unschooling movement. This type of homeschooling allows children the freedom to learn what they are interested in, to follow their own pursuits without imposed schedules or curricula. Just as children learn naturally during their first few years of life, so they will continue throughout their childhood, naturally curious and intrigued with all facets of the world. Unschooling demands a lot of trust in the child and the ability to surround him or her with stimulating, enriching resources to choose from.

So far, this had worked well with Jody. He was a lively, inquisitive child who surprised me by teaching himself how to read when he was only five. On his own initiative he would copy out the alphabet four or more times a day, in various colours, and seal it in an envelope. Donning his play postal cap, he would deliver the "letter" to me before heading off to his toys. History, science, and other traditional school subjects held a fascination for him and he threw himself wholeheartedly into the experiments we tried and the models and historical scenes we recreated. Every month we focused on a different country: finding it on the globe, cooking some of its food, visiting a restaurant, getting out a couple of books on it from the library, and doing anything else that seemed relevant. In Victoria, nature centres had microscopes available for use, the Royal BC Museum offered free admission to its excellent exhibits, and the Art Gallery had "hands-on" kid's days. There had been an endless number of group activities there for Jody to participate in. I felt it was important for a homeschooled child to experience being part of a group in which he would be instructed by someone other than me. I knew I would have to search out such activities for Jody in our new life.

The neighbours were not happy to find out that Jody was homeschooled.

"But the Lund School needs kids!" was a common refrain.

I was often in the uncomfortable position of resisting their pressure to add him to those dwindling numbers. However, we soon found out that we weren't the only Lund family whose children didn't attend school. As word spread throughout the community, we were able to connect with a handful of other homeschoolers in the Lund and Powell River area. Eventually we would form a loose homeschooling group that would meet together for fun activities like science experiments, art projects, or sports days.

Jody's classroom was now the forest. His first project was to discover what trees were on our land. A serious little biologist, he diligently matched cones to needles and gathered leaves, snipping, taping, and labelling his samples: fir, cedar, hemlock, and alder, willow, arbutus.

Jody loved to read and draw, and one day towards the end of July he came down the ladder crying, clutching a paper. He had drawn a picture of himself, with tears pouring down. Ranged around him were all the things he missed of our life in Victoria: from the tree he liked to climb, to the woolly mammoth in the museum, from the slide in the playground behind our old house, to his best friends left behind. He sobbed as if his heart would break. My sadness welled up to meet his.

"What have I done?" I thought. "I've taken him away from everything he loves." I cuddled and comforted him for a few moments, wondering how I could turn this mood around. "Okay," I said brightly, "now go back up to the loft and make a drawing of all the things you love about living here, in the forest."

He went reluctantly, but when he came down, the companion drawing showed him smiling, surrounded by many wonderful new delights he had come to love in the four weeks we'd lived in this little cabin: berries everywhere to pick and eat, snakes to catch, the pond down the hill to wade in. There were new favourite trees to climb and new friends to have fun with. Homesickness forgotten, he went happily out to play in the sunshine.

Once, he left his outdoor activities to run inside,

frightened by loud animal noises. I went out to listen, but had no idea what it was or if it was dangerous. It was a while before I happened to hear it while talking to Jeff. He smiled as he cleared up the mystery: geese were calling as they flew hidden above the trees. Just one more addition to the magic that surrounded our life in the forest, where every peaceful day overflowed with beauty. Each morning I awoke with joy to be living in the midst of nature; it truly was like permanently camping. I felt more contented than ever before.

We explored all the little trails and paths around our area. When neighbours mentioned an interesting spot, we would set out to find it. Furry often trotted along beside us on these walks. She paused occasionally to check something out, then bounded ahead of us again, startling us and eliciting our laughter. When tired of walking, she disappeared into the bushes. On our way back home, there she would be, near the spot we had last seen her, slipping onto the trail to join us again.

When we walked farther north on Baggi Road, we found an old dirt road that nature had crowded into a wide trail. The neighbours called it the Finnish Homestead Road, although little sign remained of the pioneers' house that had given it that name. In the wet time of the year, part of this road would be enveloped by swamp, but that summer we followed it up and around, past the cattails and bulrushes at its edge, coming at last in a surprise circuitous route out into the village of Lund.

Farther north still, we discovered a beautiful waterfall opposite Gilpin Road. We could hear it from Baggi Road, but had to bushwhack to find ourselves at its lovely edge, admiring the rushing white water cascading in a pleasant roar over rocks and wedged branches at its lip. Jody liked to scamper across its top ledge, stepping carefully over its flowing streams and laughing at its cooling spray. It was always fun to throw twigs or leaves in at the top and cheer them down the chutes. This quickly became our favourite hike.

Up Gilpin Road we came across two pretty little hidden lakes, Black Lake with its dark, dark water, and Trout Lake with its leaping fish. Both had huge logs wide enough to walk on, either along its edges or stretching out into deep water, like natural docks. A dilapidated cabin sagged in the bush near one of them, abandoned decades before. Who could have lived there or for what purpose had it been built? It didn't look safe and whenever we visited the lakes I warned Jody to give it a wide berth.

The days we had to leave our idyllic surroundings and head into town were centered around scheduled activities. Appointments and other town commitments could not always be arranged on the same day. We could not afford the gas to drive to Powell River more than once a week, so if we had to come in more often, we would hitchhike. This usually entailed walking two kilometres into the village of Lund to the highway where we could stick out our thumbs in the hope of a ride. We didn't have much trouble getting to town, but returning home was more difficult. Since many people heading north lived between Powell River and Lund, it would usually take us several rides to get to where we could walk home. I felt safer hitchhiking with Jody, and people seemed quick to stop when they saw a young child.

Ken, the man who had lived in the cabin before us, surprised me by coming to remove the junk he had left piled beside it. He was big and seemed a bit rough. I was slightly nervous to have a wild-looking man poking around and my heart leapt into my throat when he started shouting and swearing. I timidly peeked out the window, only to see him yelling and jumping around violently. Then he suddenly tore down the hill and out of sight. I hoped he wouldn't come back, but a few hours later he was knocking at my door. He explained how he had uncovered a hidden wasp nest. I was so relieved that there was a logical explanation that didn't include psychosis!

Every day for a week or more Ken was back, fighting the wasps. They seemed to be winning the war for awhile and I was now more frightened by the angry buzzing than his curses and erratic movements. Eventually the nest was conquered. Jody and I were fascinated by the intricate giant hive that they built inside a rolled-up sheepskin under an abandoned mattress.

Furry adapted amazingly well to life in the forest. I could scarcely believe what a ratter she turned out to be. Ken uncovered a rat's nest in an old canning jar. The babies were about the size of mice and unable to climb out. How could I get rid of them? I called Furry, our rat exterminator extraordinaire, and tipped them out on the dirt road. She dispatched almost all of them, quite the feat as they scattered in all directions. Her final catch she gave to little Pirate, who had been excitedly observing the show. Then she lay down to watch. Every time the rat would get away from Pirate, Furry would leap into action, catch it and return it to him. Feline homeschooling at its best.

Pirate in the grass by the old cabin

I gave a sigh of relief and headed out to refill the water

bucket. There was a well at the bottom of the hill, near Dan's sauna. It was an open well, a four foot circle of deep, deep water with crumbly dirt sides. It was wonderful to find water close by, though I felt like the opposite of Jill as I walked down the hill to fetch a pail of water, then laboriously lugged the full pail back up. I was pleased to have access to it, but also frightened of it. Getting out of the well, should anyone fall in, appeared impossible. As the summer progressed, the water level receded and the danger increased. Soon I had to lean way down into it to reach the water. Eventually I had to tie a rope to the bucket and throw it down to the water, a task made more difficult because the plastic bucket floated. Sometimes I could throw it in such a way that it sank, but more often than not I needed a long pole or branch to tip the floating bucket and allow it to fill.

Dan was horrified one day as he chanced upon my struggles on the lip of the well. With his arms crossed against his chest, he shook his head at my recklessness. He firmly suggested I should at least tie a rope around the nearest tree and leave the end dangling into the well. That way I would have a chance of pulling myself out should I fall in. Of course I would! I wondered why I hadn't thought of that.

The neighbours were eager to tell the story of a five-year-old boy who drowned in an old well some years before.

"He was only out of sight for fifteen minutes," they kept repeating, "when he was found floating face down."

I was terrified. Though Jody roamed at will around the cabin, I impressed upon him the potentially fatal danger of the well. He was strictly forbidden to go anywhere near it by himself, but was allowed to accompany me. He considered it a "wishing well," and though I didn't think pennies should be in our drinking water, we both threw in little stones to make our wishes. My wish for a country guy had yet to materialize. I had met lots of interesting men, even gone out with a few of them, but had so far failed to find the love I longed for. I hung on to the hope as another stone splashed into the deep water.

Several of the neighbours suggested the well ought to be filled in, but no one wanted to take responsibility for doing it. I agreed, but was in no hurry to see it happen. Not while it was my only water source.

5. The Forgotten Road

Before having a safe source of water, I would need to complete the huge project I had set myself—to build a house on my own land. The first important decision was where exactly it would go. Peter originally owned the whole twelve and a half acres and made a large garden in the centre of it. When Jeff and Darcie bought a half share, it was their obvious choice to build their house right there, next to the developed garden. I felt squeezed out. If they lived practically in the middle, where could my half be?

I looked down by Baggi Road, where there were power and phone lines. Jeff had cleared a small area bounded by two driveways and a road. He built a shed there, and installed a freezer and a telephone. I added my own phone, with a message machine; hang-ups always made me laugh, since I would never be there to answer its ring. Jeff suggested I could build my house there and offered to sell me the shed. Jody and I lounged in the sun nearby while I considered the idea. It didn't sit right. I didn't purchase over six acres in the middle of nowhere to be confined to a quarter acre bounded on three sides by roads and driveways. However, there seemed to be no way to access the back end of the property.

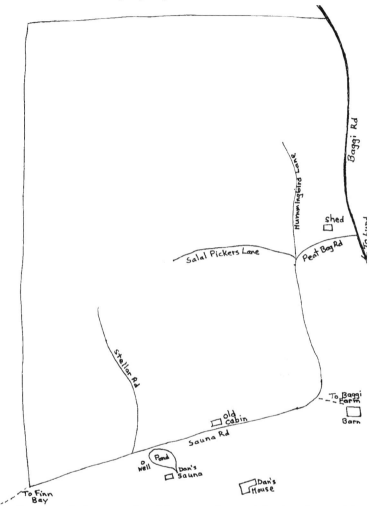

I was sitting at the big wooden table in the cabin, studying old hand-drawn maps, when I suddenly caught my breath. I blinked, staring again at the obscure road marked on only one of them. 'Stellar Road' looked like it might traverse Martin and Janet's property into the back part of mine. I dropped everything and excitedly set off looking for it, but was deflated when it didn't seem to exist. I went door-to-door, but none of the neighbours had heard of a road there. One of them, Neil, told me the way to find an overgrown road was to look for alders, the first trees to grow in a cleared area. If I could find a patch of alders around there, he advised, I should push into the bush behind and see if they continued. If they marched off in a continual line, I would have located an old road.

It worked perfectly. The alders led me on and on, up a gentle slope and way back into the bush. Surely they must reach to where my property began. I cut a small trail among them and explored around. I was looking for a natural clearing for my future house and I found three such clearings up there, all to the left of Stellar Road. Any of them might work for my house site. The first was the nicest, but also the least likely to be on my property. Next I needed to have the land surveyed so I could find out where Stellar Road crossed into my piece, if it did at all. I fervently hoped that at least one of those potential house sites would be part of my land.

I was curious about who else had known about this forgotten road. Who had named it? Why was it named after the stars? Or should it have been "Steller" after the jays? It was Peter who solved the mystery. He had discovered the overgrown road and named it for the steller's jay that squawked out a warning when he first explored its tangle. So it should have really been spelled "Steller Road!" Peter purposely included it on the map, making it one of the roads all of us tenants-in-common could access, so that it could be used to reach the back of his property, which had now become mine. He was delighted that his decision was proving correct. Although he wouldn't personally benefit, he rubbed his hands in glee at the fact that his plan had come to fruition with me. I would always call my long driveway "Steller Road" and in fact named my future house "Steller Place."

Kim came to do the surveying. He was the bearded,

bush-whacking surveyor that all the neighbours used to plot their boundaries. He cheerily found the corner posts and metal markers. He measured out half of Peter's property, but there was a problem. The half-way line came too close to Jeff and Darcie's house; in fact it cut off part of their garden. Luckily, Kim had a solution. If my half included a panhandle all the way out to Baggi Road, I could use it to run power or phone lines through to my house site. The resulting triangle-shaped piece with long handle would no longer crowd into Jeff and Darcie's living space. We all agreed on that border, and Kim cut a slash along it and tied orange surveyor's tape. Now we could walk the borders, through previously inaccessible tangles of bush and fallen trees.

Jody and I delighted in exploring this new, rough trail. In some places the forest through which it strode was dark and silent; in others sunlight filtered through and huckleberries nodded enticingly. We found a lovely hidden clearing warm in the sunshine and full of the lacey white heads of yarrow. The Yarrow Clearing wasn't far from our house site and quickly became a favourite picnic spot. Farther on, the border slash climbed up a rocky bit till we suddenly found ourselves on the edge of a moss-covered cliff, with natural stone steps we could carefully pick our way down. We dubbed this Mossy Mountain, a secret hidden spot with soft covered rocks to sit on and strange acoustics. We could hear people talking as if they were right beside us, but no one ever noticed our shouted replies.

To my relief, Steller Road did indeed extend into my piece. The boundary Kim marked crossed right through the second of the three clearings that I had found, leaving only the farthest one available for a house site. It was mostly level, with huge flat slabs of rock and a number of gorgeous arbutus trees, twisting and curving like sinuous forest sculptures.

There was a large sunny depression, now growing

small-to-medium-sized cedar trees, to the south of the clearing. It looked suitable for my long-awaited garden. Aware that it takes newly planted fruit trees years before they produce anything edible, I was anxious to plant some as soon as possible. I took the time to put in apple and pear trees, as well as a gooseberry bush, around the edge of this projected garden area, ignoring the cedar trees for the moment.

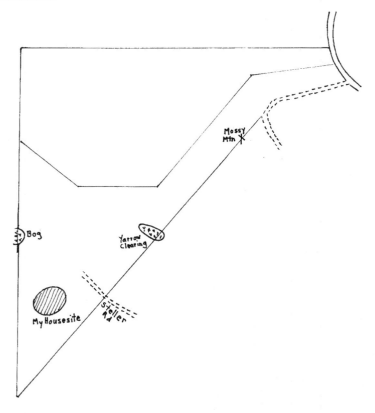

Before I could do more, a driveable road had to reach the site. This meant negotiating with Martin, the neighbour who owned the cabin I was staying in and whose land the road would traverse. This was difficult. He had seen people come and go and was certain a single woman from the city wouldn't last long. Why should he allow a road through his pristine land when I would soon give up and move away? I smiled inwardly at this; he had no idea how stubborn I was.

In the end, it was the news that I had planted fruit trees that swayed him. He took that as a sign that I planned to stay long term. He agreed to let me clear and use the road if I would pay him $100. The trees I could keep for firewood. Done deal! Though my hoarded money was dwindling, Jeff and Darcie split the cost of some big loppers with me, and I cleared away all the salal, salmonberries, and other brush. I am only five feet tall and weighed just ninety-one pounds, so it was a major workout for me. Then I purchased a small used chainsaw from Kolezar's, a power equipment store in town. Bob, who lived down on Craig Road, gave me lessons on its use and safety. One by one, the alders came crashing down, each one frightening in its own way. I was conscious of the power and danger inherent in the chainsaw. There was a certain amount of relief each time that I switched it off, if only to sharpen the chain, which had to be done often. Sometimes a falling tree would get hung up in standing ones nearby, occasionally meriting several more cuts before it would fall free. I swallowed frustration, ignored my quaking heart, and persevered.

Eventually they were all down and bucked for firewood. Now I was faced with a road full of stumps. I was told I needed a "skidder" and given a phone number. Al, the driver, wasn't free for a few weeks. While waiting, I turned my attention to the potential garden area I had discovered to the south of my house site. Chainsaw in hand, I cleared the mostly small cedar trees from this area, leaving the stumps scattered among what would become the raised beds, and the felled trees tossed to the side. There was little soil anywhere around the site; like most of Lund, it was all rock. Neighbours explained that the heavy coastal rains washed any soil down into the bogs. Kim's survey showed that my western boundary went through one of these bogs, a smallish one not far from the house site. I used the loppers to cut a trail from the garden site to the bog. I still had enough money to purchase a wheelbarrow, which I trundled up to the shallow marsh.

The future garden area

It was quiet and peaceful on the edge of this bog, the swampy water dark and still. As I contemplated the serenity, I was suddenly startled by the raucous call of a bald eagle. Its hoarse creaking was reminiscent of the screech of a rusty clothesline pulley. There was an eagle's nest hidden somewhere far up among the many branches of towering evergreens nearby. I loved to hear the harsh clamour of the eagles and thrilled to see them soar effortlessly ever higher in majestic circles.

It was a lot of work digging out the peat and carting it by wheelbarrow over to the garden site, where I could then shift it onto each bed of branches, twigs, and leaves to make the type of layered garden I had first seen at Kurt's in

Yahk so long before. I quickly learned how to get the most out of one trip without making the wheelbarrow overly heavy. Sweaty work. My muscles ached, but bed by bed the garden grew.

When Al finally came, his skidder easily uprooted the stumps along Steller Road. He asked me about putting down gravel. The ground itself seemed gravely and when I told him I didn't intend to put any down, he stared in disbelief at my naivety.

"Won't be much of a road if you don't," he said tersely. "Come the rains, it'll be mud too deep to drive through."

Oh.

Gravel was laid in September and the road was complete. It was exciting to have finished this early step in my plans and to be able to drive to my house site.

6. Rising to the Top

Before I could do anything further, we had to head down to Vancouver for Duncan and Monica's wedding. Jody had a special part to play: as the groom's son, he was to lead the wedding march. He walked solemnly behind the bagpiper, through Common Ground Housing Co-op, where Duncan's mother, Betty, lived, to their Common Room. There a pre-nuptial dinner party was to take place. The actual wedding was a small private affair, but this dinner party included all the family and friends of the bride and groom. It featured a "Family Music and Song Recital." As part of this program, Duncan asked Jody to sing a song, which he could choose. He climbed on a chair and led everyone in a spirited rendition of what he called "The Exercise Song" *(One Finger, One Thumb, Keep Moving)*. The entire gathering dissolved into laughter as they attempted to keep up with all the movements and sounds. It warmed my heart to see Jody included in the start of Duncan's new life and I was proud of his fearless singing in front of the crowd. It was a bittersweet moment, as I tried to rise above my own disappointment and be happy for the wonderful man who meant so much to me.

We returned to Lund just in time for Jody's seventh birthday. It was a beautiful sunny day. He opened his presents in the old cabin before we headed to Cranberry Lake in town. The Wildlife Sanctuary was closed, but that didn't stop us from feeding the squawking ducks, geese, and one lone seagull. When our bag of bread crumbs was depleted, we headed around the lake to the playground and the sandy shore, where Jody climbed the huge boulder at the water's edge and stood triumphantly upon its top. We ate lunch at the Bowman Kafé, then were off to a "Penny-a-Pound" photographer. Jody posed grinning beside a contrived old wagon wheel, a gap showing his missing front teeth and his long hair covering his ears.

We stopped at the post office for a present from Granny and Grandad in far-off Ontario, then sped home for a party. Jody's six new friends hunted for peanuts in the cabin, ate cake and ice cream, then played games outside for prizes.

When all had gone home, Jody and I spent the evening playing and talking until 8:45, when with a last poem, we both went to sleep, a stunning star-filled sky peeking in on us through the remaining loft window.

The next morning, I began to ask around about how I should go about moving the old cabin up to my building site. More incredulous stares. An old cabin, it would seem, cannot simply be lifted up and moved to another location. It would fall to pieces. Who knew? I thought of various ways to brace it, but all my ideas were shot down. I could find no one who was willing to even attempt it. As I absorbed this startling turn of events, another idea percolated to the fore: if I couldn't move the cabin as it was, I would take it apart and reassemble it on my land.

I was down at the well one day, mulling over this plan, when Doug came by. Doug lived at what we called Baggi Farm, a loose collection of old buildings with new transient residents, just down the other side of the hill. He had red hair and a perpetually sunburned face covered in freckles. He always struck me as soft-spoken and shy, and was rumoured to drink heavily. On that day, he strode purposefully up to me and, after only the slightest hesitation, offered to sell me his house. He had built it, he explained, in four-by-eight panels that were made to easily come apart and go back together. Baggi Farm was already the second location he had set it up in; now he was moving into town and would have no use for it. Surprised and intrigued, I went to have a look.

I had been to Baggi Farm many times before. Don lived in the main farmhouse there. Don was tall and wiry, and usually very serious. I sensed he might have a temper, but he was always very kind to me. Once he dropped by when I was in the middle of vigorously stirring bread dough and saw my wooden spoon snap in two. On the spot he promised to carve me one that wouldn't break. A few days later, true to his word, he presented me with a solid wooden spoon that survived many years of heavy use. When Don found I had no running water, he invited me to shower at Baggi Farm whenever I wished.

In all the times I had been there, I had never noticed the small trail on the far side of the barn that Doug led me to that day. We followed it to a clearing where Doug had set up his little house. It looked like a box, a simple rectangle, long and narrow, with a minimally sloped roof. It came with an aluminum screen door and four modern windows. He wanted $1,000. I told him I would consider it.

I didn't have much extra money. The Family Allowance, though less than $30 a month, easily paid for gas for my van and propane for my stove. The Child Tax Credit, which came as a lump sum of several hundred dollars each spring for claiming a dependant on my income tax return, took care of the van insurance and hopefully any repairs. When I moved from Victoria, I naively thought I wouldn't need money. I planned to live off the land. What would I need money for? I had bags of hand-me-downs in my old steamer trunk for Jody to grow into, compiled over the years from friends and acquaintances with older and bigger children, and organized by size, right up to the early teens. Surely Furry and Pirate could catch their own food. I was already experienced at growing vegetables and imagined the addition of chickens and a few fruit trees would handle our food needs. The neighbours stared, astounded at my wishful thinking. "You're going to need some money," they insisted. And it didn't take long to realize that was true.

Most of the jobs I worked at that last busy year in Victoria didn't qualify me for what we then called "UI" (Unemployment Insurance), however a few did. I hadn't bothered to apply, but my neighbour, Jeff, convinced me to give it a try. I knew it wouldn't come to much, but at least it would be some money. Once it ran out, I would be able to fall back on my old mainstay of babysitting, and in years to come I would start a Friday morning preschool at my house. For now, UI actually brought me $85 a week, which seemed more than enough before Doug's suggestion that I buy his little house.

A plan began to take form. I could continue living in the old cabin while I took down Doug's house and rebuilt it on my land. Then I could move into it while I took apart the old cabin and put it back together joined on to Doug's house. Was this possible? Could I rebuild these houses without one of their walls and make them into a single two-room-plus-loft cabin? Yes, I was told, as long as I had a big enough beam to join everything together and support the roof.

I talked Doug down to $900. I pooled my remaining money and a couple of UI cheques to pay him a few hundred down and agreed to pay off the balance at $100 a month. But I didn't want a house like a long narrow box. Sitting down with paper and pencil, I began to plan how I would shift the walls around to create the house I wanted. However, now that winter was fast approaching, with its driving rain and howling winds, putting any of my house-building ideas into motion would have to wait.

As the year turned, the dark bled into the mornings and the evenings. The silent nights were chilled and lonely. At times I felt cut off and adrift from other people. One evening the stillness of the dark was broken by unexpected headlights that slowly topped the hill and came to a stop outside the cabin. It seemed unbelievable that we had a visitor!

Sandy had made the long trek to invite me to an information session on something called EST. I had never heard of it before and it didn't sound that interesting. However, I was impressed and flattered that Sandy had gone to such effort to invite me—she even offered to babysit Jody while I attended. So I agreed, little knowing what I was getting myself into.

EST (Erhard Seminar Training) was a two weekend personal transformation workshop on empowerment and responsibility, to be held in Vancouver. It was very expensive and I was firm that I wouldn't be pressured into taking it. However, the philosophical questions raised were intriguing. I knew many of the people at this meeting and they all spoke about how EST had positively changed their lives. In fact, EST had rippled steadily through Lund over the past few years, touching more and more people. Almost all of my friends and neighbours had taken the training, and were enthusiastic in their support of it.

At the end of the meeting, we were invited to sign up for the seminar or to stay behind to ask questions. I had plenty. I challenged its necessity, its cost, and many other things, arguing animatedly with the presenters. I stayed for quite a while, till only myself and one other holdout remained. I don't recall what was said that finally convinced me— perhaps it was the subsidy they offered that would cover the cost—but to everyone's surprise, I suddenly decided to register. My capitulation spurred the other holdout to give in as well. It was late and I hurried off to collect Jody and make the long drive home.

The next afternoon, I was shocked speechless when the holdout from the previous night, Sean, showed up at my door. I was amazed and flattered that he put in the effort to find out who I was and to travel up these far back roads to search me out. Sean was an attractive fellow, with a trim black beard and crinkly laugh lines by his eyes. He seemed a gentle soul and my heart skipped a beat when he asked me out to dinner.

It was an extravagant meal. He impressed me by ordering the most expensive item on the menu, though I later found out he was spending everything he had in a successful attempt to charm me. Our conversation started well, as we eased into each other's lives and views but before the evening ended, it became more intense. I sensed disagreement when controversial topics, like assault against women, came up. Sean felt the numbers were exaggerated; I disagreed, and mentioned I too had experienced assault firsthand. Sadly, it would be our only date.

The seminars themselves were life-changing and powerful. I have strong memories of the activities and visualizations I participated in. In some ways they were gruelling: long hours with few breaks and a strict code of self-discipline. We weren't to wear watches, eat, talk, or move about. This elicited a deep focus without distractions. Many things shifted for me in those long hours: I understood my relationships with my parents in a new way, grasping reasons and causes I had never before seen, rising above petty grudges I had long held. I realized how the events of my life, in the past and going forward, were a direct result of my actions and reactions alone. This was profound and startling, a true altering of perspective.

During these long seminars, Jody stayed with his grandpa and step-grandma, Gordon and Rene. After each long day, I decompressed with them, describing my new ideas and feelings. Gordon was a retired high school teacher, bespeckled and thoughtful, intrigued at my non-stop account of the workshops and the philosophical questions they raised. Rene was a social worker, smiling and helpful. At the end, I headed back to Lund and the daunting tasks ahead strengthened and empowered, feeling in control and able to rise above the challenges and disappointments.

7. Saved by Frost, Cursed by Cold

The cabin's small tin wood stove had been mistreated. Previous tenants had built a fire directly on its thin tin bottom, forgetting the necessary bed of stones to safely isolate the metal from the scorching flames. Then they went to bed, leaving the fire to burn through the bottom of the stove and fall onto the wood floor. Only their young child, crying and coughing in the night, saved their lives and the cabin. The wood stove now stood forlorn and useless, its gaping hole irreparable. When I moved it I found that the loose sheet of plywood on which it stood covered a matching hole burnt right through the floor. What a close call for those tenants! It chilled me to think about it.

Luckily, Sean had assured me he had an old cast-iron woodstove that I could use for the winter. A *real* stove, he told me, not a flimsy tin affair, but one that you could light a fire in without fear. Though we were no longer in touch, he surprised me by dropping off the promised stove before cold weather arrived.

I had to buy new stovepipe for it, a beautiful, clean, black stovepipe, cool and smooth to the touch. It was a happy purchase, but my smile soon faded. I pulled and pushed, squeezed and shoved and forced, but no matter what I tried, I could not get the pipe to fit into the stove opening. My hands were raw, my arms ached, and after several days I collapsed into sobs.

"I can't do it, it's no good, I just can't do it," I wailed in despair as Jody looked on forlornly, barely holding back his own tears.

Then he was urgently touching my arm, "Someone's coming!"

Stifling my sobs, I heard voices! After weeks of seeing no one, three lost hikers chose that moment to walk past my cabin. Hastily wiping my tears, I ran outside to ask for help. In ten minutes the strong young men had the stovepipe in the stove and were on their way in the right direction, leaving me smiling and giggling with relief, embarrassed to have broken down in front of Jody.

I don't recall who or why, but someone dropped off a load of firewood. The stove was top-loading, the large, oval lid sliding ponderously aside for stoking. Once the fire was burning well, all the smoke was sucked up the stovepipe that served as our chimney, but if it was only smouldering, a blast of acrid smoke would hit me in the face when I tried to add wood.

Winter came early in 1984. Jody shivered in the red tights of his devil costume as he trick-or-treated at the few houses there were up Edmondson Road in the village of Lund. After he had exhausted all possibilities there, we were relieved to duck into the warmth of the Lund Community Centre for the children's Halloween party. The hall was packed with high-spirited ghosts and pirates, bobbing for apples and sipping hot chocolate, while their parents complimented each other on their children's creative costumes. When the party was over, no one was prepared for the shocking sight that appeared when the door was opened. Snow! A deluge of large whirling snowflakes was fast accumulating over the road, the cars, and the rooftops. There was a rush to get up the Lund hill before it was impassable, but for many it was too late. Jody and I walked carefully up the steep slope to the sound of spinning tires, glad that we parked at the top near the street that had shelled out Jody's treats.

Halloween 1984

There was still snow on the ground a week into November. The old cabin in the forest had no electricity, no running water, no telephone, and no insulation in the bare plywood walls. The winter morning was cold and frosty, both outside and in. Shivering, I scrambled down the ladder from the sleeping loft, my breath visible in the frigid air, my teeth clamped against the numbing temperature. There was ice on the cats' water dish. Jody was still asleep in the loft. I hurried to start the wood stove, talking quietly with the neighbour's two little girls, Terra and Shanti, who had slept over. They complained they were cold. Then we all felt the warmth relax us as we stretched our hands out to the welcome heat. Suddenly a startling light came from upstairs, where no light could possibly exist.

The stovepipe passed through an opening in the floor upstairs and on out of the bare plywood roof to become our chimney. In the dim early morning, the sudden bright light streamed down the opening, gleaming on the dull black of the wood stove, exactly as if someone had flicked a switch.

Our conversation faltered and we all looked up. I stood and peered through the opening, confused, but could see nothing unusual.

"I think he just turned on the light," Terra said hopefully.

"There is no light," was my terse reply. And there was no response to my questioning call to my son. "Stay here," I added to the girls on my way to the ladder.

Poking my head into the loft, I took in Jody's still sleeping form at one end and, the length of the cabin away from him, a flickering flame burning through the ceiling at the other. Fear clutched at me. I pushed it aside, remembering that there was water in the kettle downstairs and lots more in my five gallon container. I raced down for the kettle and back up to splash its contents up on the visible flame. The fire hissed at my efforts and continued undeterred.

"What are you doing?" came the tremulous voice of my son.

My mind swirled. This wasn't going to work. The fire was on the topside of the roof. I couldn't put it out from inside.

I shooed Jody down the ladder in front of me and ordered the children to go outside and stay there. One look around back confirmed my predicament. Tall trees crowded the cabin, but none I could climb. I tried throwing water at the roof, but it was a useless waste of a precious commodity. I needed help. I thought of my only close neighbour, Dan, who lived by the pond just down the hill.

Dan was quiet and kept to himself, not at all sociable, but always friendly to me. At times I heard him playing guitar or cutting bush and moving huge rocks like some kind of superhuman machine.

Tearing back around the cabin, I noticed the children standing obediently outside, the girls coatless and shivering, their bare feet on the frosted ground. I instructed them to grab their coats and boots from just inside the door, then to wait with the cats in the van parked across the small road.

The trees beside the road were a blur as I ran down the steep incline faster than I had thought possible, screaming Dan's name over and over.

His cabin looked deserted; my yells only amplified the stillness that greeted me. No! I bounded up his steps still screaming his name and pounded with both my fists on his door, my heart refusing to accept what my mind had already grasped. Silence. Despair threatened to engulf me.

As I turned away, he finally called out, "What is it? What's wrong?"

Relief washed over me.

"My cabin—the roof's on fire!"

And I tore back up the hill, my breath ragged and a pain stabbing my side.

I checked on the children, then waited impatiently for my reclusive neighbour to arrive, while fearfully monitoring the fire's ominous progress. After several anxious moments, I was relieved to see him hurrying up the hill with two huge pots of water from his pond. I took him around the back to show him the stubborn flame creeping along the frosty plywood.

"It doesn't look bad," he reassured me, "but we need a ladder. Do you have one?"

No, I didn't own a ladder—but wait, there was one up to the loft, a massive wooden one that I feared was nailed in place. I ran for it and giving a mighty jerk, pulled it free.

Had it just been leaning there? I grabbed the middle of it and ran back to Dan, who placed it firmly against the house. I handed up pots of water and he poured them on the flame until, with much hissing, steam, and smoke, the fire was defeated, the crisis averted.

Afterward, we talked about it all, decompressing—something burning must have landed on the roof from the chimney.

"Your chimney should be higher," he advised, "and not just made of stovepipe."

It was hard to explain why the fire had not engulfed the roof. Saved by the heavy frost, we conjectured. Strangely enough, I had to ask my invaluable neighbour to carry the wooden ladder and place it back in its regular spot. That ladder, that I heaved aside and ran around the house with, I now found too heavy to even lift. It's amazing what adrenalin can do.

Our Christmas Tree

Christmas came soon after, and our firewood was almost gone. It seemed strange to think back on the previous Christmas, when we had spent the last of our money to purchase a tree in the city. Now we owned a whole forest of trees to choose from. We selected a little fir growing near the cabin, stood it in a bucket of stones, and decorated it, the dove of peace on the top and Jody's homemade ornaments gracing its spindly branches. Jody threaded popcorn and cranberries into long garlands to wrap around the tree. A previous year's pressurized can of spray-on snow and unused templates jollied up the cabin windows with bells and stars. I managed to bake gingerbread house pieces in the tiny propane stove and laboriously whipped the egg white icing by hand. My arm ached so that I despaired of being able to keep going until they would form into stiff enough peaks to mimic snow and hang over the eaves like icicles. Could that even be done by hand? I felt triumphant when I finally succeeded. Once the walls and roof were covered in the shiny white snow icing, Jody's old stash of Halloween candy could be put to use. He carefully arranged all the bright, colourful, untasted sweets to complete our most gorgeous Christmas decoration.

I found an ancient school desk with attached seat and painted it bright green and yellow. And I purchased a large old typewriter for him. But Jody wanted only one thing for Christmas that year: an indoor toilet. How could I come up with an indoor toilet? Then one day, in a second-hand store in town, I came across a fold-up metal frame with an attached toilet seat, and bags that fit underneath. Not quite what Jody had in mind, but an indoor toilet nonetheless, and Christmas Day, as it should be, was filled with surprises and laughter.

Boxing Day found us walking down to the beach far below our property, known as Diver's Rock for its painted scuba sign indicating hidden interest deep under the waves. We brought bread crumbs to feed the delighted seagulls, who swooped and splashed as they noisily fought for their post-Christmas treats. Jody strove to throw crumbs to the timid ones who stayed back and we cheered whenever one of the shyer gulls or a brave little duck managed to grab a crumb. This was the start of a Boxing Day tradition that we would continue for years.

Working at his new desk

Our gingerbread bird feeder

When the Christmas tree came down, Jody climbed on top of the van to drape the strings of cranberries and popcorn over tree branches across from our cabin, so the little birds could celebrate as well. I pulled off one side of the small roof of our homemade gingerbread house, and Jody filled it with birdseed. I helped him add this edible bird feeder to the top of the van. Then we sat in the loft and enjoyed all the twittering excitement, so soft and musical compared to the harsh calls of the waterfowl.

The weather up here seemed strangely localized, with little pockets of surprises. When we walked to the village of Lund, there might be puddles along a road, then rounding a corner we would suddenly find ice. I liked to trek up to look at my building site once a day, to feel the hope and promise of Steller Place, our future home. Some days it would be raining at my house site, yet snowing at Jeff and Darcie's, only a few minutes' walk away. In fact, Jody was greatly disappointed to learn that our projected place always received less snow than anywhere else around the neighbourhood, a fact that delighted me. We joked that we would live in the tropics of Lund. In years to come, our tomatoes would ripen a full three weeks ahead of tomatoes in Jeff and Darcie's garden, sitting as it did in a hollow where cold air seemed to loiter. My site was at the top of a hill, where sunshine warmed the rocks and where trees protected us from ocean breezes.

Another load of firewood had arrived, but this was wet. Soaked in fact. On New Year's Eve we burned the last of the dry firewood, and our troubles began in earnest. It was all but impossible to get the fire started. The cold closed in around us, a numbing, all-encompassing cold that surpassed uncomfortable and edged towards frightening. Sitting up in bed, we could see our breaths, white vapour hanging for an instant in the crisp air. Icy tears of frustration shivered down my cheeks. The very air was smoky, yet the wood stove stood stubbornly frigid, refusing to light. Our clothes and hair smelled continually of smoke. I would hold my breath, avert my eyes, and quickly throw on a log, which would hiss and spit and pop. Eventually, hopefully, it would dry out enough to burn. Some mornings the only heat in the uninsulated cabin came from cooking porridge on the little propane stove.

Snow blanketed the hills from time to time and beautified our frigid surroundings. Small snowmen peeked out of the bush near the cabin. We never saw raccoons during the day, but snowy mornings displayed the tracks of their night-time adventures. The bald tires on the van meant we often had to park at the bottom of the hill and make our way up its slippery slope on foot, sometimes packing groceries. Somehow we made it through January, through the tears, the smoke, and the chills.

By the end of that month, I'd had enough. It had been a long time since I had visited my parents in Ontario. Though February often shows its blizzard teeth back east, I knew my parents' house would be warm and cozy. When they offered to pay for our flights, I left my cares behind and flew out of Vancouver the first of February. I visited my sister up in Mount Forest and Jody tobogganed with his cousins. He reconnected with more cousins at my brother's. My parents even took us to Niagara Falls. We stayed with them the entire month and I returned to our cabin recharged.

Thankfully spring had arrived before us. March began warm and clean; the air smelled sweet and flowers began to show their cheery colours. A magical spring event was taking place up and down the coast. From the Lund dock, we watched in awe as billions of tiny herring filled the waters to spawn. Their sides flashed with silver in the sunlight and the salt water near shore took on a greenish hue. What an enchanting abundance of aquatic life was returning to signal the change of season! This miraculous event marked the beginning of an annual spring rite, which we would look forward to throughout the long winters. Little did we know that overfishing would doom this performance after only three more springs; then it would be more than thirty years before herring returned here to spawn again.

We were delighted to have made it through our first winter in the country. Every week seemed easier than the last. Finally, with renewed energy, I could get out once again and start working on our new house.

8. Down to the Ground

The sun beat down upon me from a cloudless sky, a forget-me-not blue edged with the comforting green of towering evergreens. I was on the slightly sloped roof of what was now my own little house, purchased from Doug. It would become my living room when reassembled on my land. First it had to be disassembled.

In my hand was my new favourite tool. My neighbour, Jeff, had called it a cat's claw. It fit comfortably in my palm, like a mini crowbar. I delighted in lining it up next to a nail, pounding it into the wood with my hammer, and prying out the nail as easily as if I was pulling out a thumbtack. It was fun, like playing a game. As relaxing as pulling and poking a lump of clay. Like the proverbial elephant that can be eaten one bite at a time, I knew how to dismantle a whole house: one nail at a time.

I liked being up on the roof, but ladders always made me nervous. Every time I needed to go up there or back down, I had to take a deep breath, swallow consciously, and steel myself. Once on the firm solidity of the roof, it was fine to be high up among the trees. They stood even higher, so I couldn't see beyond the edges of the clearing. A hawk called from the top of one fir, and I paused to watch two squirrels chase each other around and through the dense branches of another, chittering as they went.

Jody played nearby. I could hear him as I worked and would call out to him if his chatter ceased. I saved the nails as I pulled them out, determined to reuse any I could. If I dropped a nail, I would shout to Jody to find it, and he would diligently stop his play and search, usually discovering it and putting it in a little container. When all the nails had been removed from a piece of plywood, I would have Jody stand far back while I slowly slid it off the edge of the roof and lowered it down. Then I would remove the rafters that had supported it. As the roof decreased in size, I moved along it, till I was on the last plywood sheet. The final nail had to be removed while I stood on the worrisome ladder, hanging on to the top of the wall.

It was a dream April that year, an April as warm and dry as summer. It was my first April in Lund and I had no reason to think it might be unusual weather. When sweat trickled down my back, I removed my shirt and, never one to wear a bra, worked topless, confident in the isolation of Doug's clearing, totally unselfconscious: the normalcy of naturism in the midst of nature.

One by one the wall panels came down and I piled each on top of the others. Every panel, every board, I had marked with letters, so I could plan how to put them back together, exactly the way I helped Jody build his models: B fits between A and C. I was lucky. It was obvious how this house came apart and just as obvious how to put it back together. I didn't need any kind of specialized knowledge about house construction to simply reverse the process and put back up what I was taking down.

The counter and shelves had to be removed along with the walls. Then the plywood flooring had to be pried up. Last of all the foundation beams and the small cement blocks they rested on were taken down and neatly stacked to one side. Looking around the clearing, I felt so pleased to have accomplished this task and eager to begin the next. That night I baked a cake, and Jody and I celebrated in the old cabin where we were still living.

There were little kittens in the old cabin now. Furry gave birth to her first Lund litter on the fourth of April. I was a little wary of her older kitten, Pirate, now grown into a handsome tom. I had heard that male cats might kill kittens, but my fears proved groundless. If Furry was off hunting, Pirate would jump in the box to kittensit, conscientiously washing his charges and purring loudly when they snuggled into his soft striped fur to sleep. Furry would bound back in to nurse her kits, and as they got older, she would bring a dead mouse or rat for them to check out.

One warm afternoon in the middle of May, Furry walked in with a dead rat that she proceeded to eat while the largest of the kittens sniffed it and tentatively licked. It wasn't long after that they both became violently ill. The kitten recovered, but Furry did not. And just like that, a light went out in our life. The steadfast little cat who had shared so many adventures and travelled the province with us, who had kept our surrounding area free of rodents, who had purred and cuddled her way intertwined with our lives throughout the previous exciting years, was gone.

We held a service for Furry with songs, poems, and shared memories, both Jody and I speaking through our tears. We buried her nearby, with a grave marker and plantings. It seemed so fortuitous that the kittens had turned six weeks old the day before, just barely old enough to eat cat food. Pirate now became a surrogate mother to them, and his attention and care were heart-warming to see. I was deeply shaken that a dear cat could be gone so suddenly, and in a frenzy of over-reaction, I decided to keep the entire litter. Jody named the black and white female Chinny, for her black chin. I called the little male tabby Striper. The tiniest, a nondescript black and white became known as Plain Jane.

Jane was more than just tiny. She didn't seem able to adapt to life in the bush. Her meow was more of a croak, and she cried a lot, piteously. She didn't play with the other two, or join in Jody's kitten-enticing games. What to do with her? As the weeks passed, I came to the sad conclusion that she shouldn't stay with us, yet I couldn't imagine how to find a home for her.

The solution presented itself on one of our town days. We had recently discovered Animal World and it became one of our regular stops in Powell River. Jody and I both thrilled to see all the bright coloured fishes, the tiny swimming turtles, the chirping birds, and a myriad other little creatures. However, the main attraction by far was the huge colourful parrot who stood on a bar in the front of the store. If a customer said "Hello" to him, he would answer back. If you were lucky, he would ask "How are you?" and say other assorted phrases. Jody adored him and loved to try and elicit his speech. And to visit with the occasional puppies or kittens for sale there. That gave me an idea. Would Animal World take Jane?

It would indeed, if I paid $3.00 for upkeep and if I agreed to take her back if she didn't sell. So with a heavy heart, I took little, croaking Jane to town and placed her in a large open box, full of cat toys and goodies. It was hard to leave her there, and I was near tears as we drove back to Lund without her.

Every town day, I sent Jody to check if she was still there, afraid to go in myself lest he demand I take her back. It took a few weeks, but finally the day came that Jody reported Jane was gone. Relief coursed through me. I was anxious for information about the person who had bought her.

"It was a woman who felt sorry for her," the man behind the counter grinned.

Poor little Jane. I hoped she would have an easier life in town.

Back in Lund, while Chinny and Striper, under the watchful eye of Pirate, entertained Jody with their adorable antics, I continued the work on our land. The next step would be to assemble the house/living room and move into it, so I could dismantle the old cabin. Neighbours rolled their eyes at my plans, but I stubbornly pushed ahead. Several tried to discourage me, but nothing they said convinced me it couldn't be done.

It was around that time that one evening an unexpected visitor dropped by, bringing a fresh-caught salmon. I met Prem the previous year, at the Healing Gathering up Powell Lake, one of the red-clothed Rajneesh followers. I got to know him quite well, having run into him fairly often around Lund. He was kind and easy-going, soft-spoken with a delicate French accent. I considered him a good friend. I appreciated the salmon he offered me, but having no way to keep it, I invited him to stay for supper to help eat it up. He no longer dressed in red and explained to me how he had left the group after the guru, Rajneesh, was convicted of criminal activities. Prem's real name was Yvon and I found it very difficult to suddenly switch the name I had always known him by. Yet conversation flowed easily, long after Jody had been tucked into bed up in the loft. It was a lovely evening, stars carpeting the dark, and crickets and frogs chorusing together. When Yvon finally got up to leave, I invited him instead to stay. With no privacy in the little cabin, we decided to sleep in the van parked out front. I checked on Jody, sleeping blissfully unaware up above, and we silently slipped across to the van.

I planned to be back in the cabin before Jody awoke, but the sun was barely up when I heard him call. He stood forlornly in the cabin doorway wearing his pyjamas, a worried frown troubling his young features. I hurried to slide open the window at the head of our bed and reassure him, waking Yvon in the process.

"Why did you sleep in the van?" he asked innocently.

I stumbled out a reply, trying to come up with an answer he could understand. I was horrified to hear he woke up in the night and cried, noticing that I was missing. In his childish imagination, he thought I must have walked Yvon back to where he parked and been killed by a bear!

He begged me not to do that again, and feeling guilty for having caused him such anguish, I promised. The next time Yvon spent the night, Jody would have a sleepover at Terra and Shanti's, which also happened to be when he got his first tick. Darcie removed the offending parasite and I was appalled to see the small chunk of missing skin on his back where the little nasty had implanted.

In the ensuing months, Yvon would come over from time to time, helping on the house, visiting and laughing, spending the night. I so enjoyed his company, but it was sadly obvious from the beginning that my future was not tied to his. Yvon was clear and adamant—he did not want children. I was just as firm and definite that I did.

Yvon's visits were sporadic and most of the time I was on my own working on the house or figuring out what needed to be done. At this point, I was uncertain what to do next. In fact, I was stumped. My building site was about a kilometre from Doug's clearing. I assumed I could transport all the pieces of the dismantled house in my van. When I backed up to the piles of panels and plywood, it was obvious not one of them could possibly fit. Now what would I do?

9. Bungled Beginnings, Helping Hands

I put the transportation puzzle aside and began preparatory work on the spot where I would build.

Ready to start

I had chosen a natural clearing as my house site. A large flat slab of rock would serve as a patio of sorts. Beside it, I carefully measured out the size of the floor, rearranging the walls of the original rectangle to give me a firewood porch and an extension that I hoped to enclose in glass for an attached greenhouse. I fit it all in between the towering trees in the hope of not having to fell any of them.

The brush was easily cleared away. Though I had no idea how to transport the large panels up to the site, I loaded the cement blocks and dragged the huge heavy beams over to my van. Getting them in was tricky, and they extended well beyond the rear doors. Then I slowly drove through the potholes and over the bumps, up and down the hills to my site, where I dragged each beam into place. My small body was growing stronger.

My building site was not level but I knew those massive foundation beams had to be. I was making a post and beam foundation, by cutting posts and standing them on the cement blocks. When I had used all the cement blocks, I mixed and poured concrete to stand the remaining posts on. The beams stretched from post to post and had to be level in all directions, which wasn't easy to achieve.

I was delighted to have a level. I don't recall where it came from, but I found it indispensable. It was a long, lightweight aluminum tool, with cheerful floating yellow bubbles. If a bubble lined up exactly between the lines, all was true and level. It was a bit fiddly to make a beam level, with many adjustments and readjustments to the height of the posts. Then boards laid from beam to beam also had to be level, which meant re-levelling what had previously been perfectly even. As the days passed, my frustration increased.

It was a slow process and not without tears. My wrists and shoulders began to ache, but I persevered. Jody held one end of each beam on its post, while I lifted the other end into place. Between times, he played near the clearing.

There were cedar trees with low branches he could climb and an arbutus tree that grew in the shape of a natural bench, where we sat to eat our lunch.

And that's when it all went wrong. A beam that was level before lunch, was not level after lunch. How could that be? What had changed? Confused and upset, I took some calming breaths and made adjustments. But the mystery persisted. Would I ever get everything level? Why was it so difficult? It seemed that I would never complete this step. It was like a magic trick: now they were level, now they weren't.

Over the course of several days, I slid towards hopelessness. I noticed that one of the supposedly level beams didn't look level at all. That's when it dawned on me: the level I was using was not accurate. In fact, its two edges gave two different readings.

Fortunately it contained many bubbles and I determined that, as long as I laid it with the good edge up, it would read true. At last I could confidently level the foundation in all directions!

Jeff had a piano and offered to teach Jody some music. He enjoyed this and soon asked to join the Apprentice Choir in Powell River, a precursor to the Academy Boy's Choir. He had to audition to be accepted into the choir and, not being able to carry a tune myself, I was pleasantly surprised when he demonstrated the ability to vocally match notes played on the piano. Jeff was pleased. It was when we were at his house for Jody's piano lesson that I proudly announced my success with the foundation.

Jeff immediately suggested I hold a house-raising party.

"Buy a case of beer and invite everyone to help build your house."

What a great idea! I thought maybe four people could carry a panel up and over the hills to my building site, but Jeff dismissed such a notion. Instead he called someone he knew with a flat deck truck to transport them. The problem I had agonized over for weeks was solved in an instant.

I used his phone to call my friends and our other neighbours. I lettered huge cardboard signs directing people to the house-raising, and placed them at each turn along the maze of back roads leading to my site.

The weather continued dry and warm. Now well into June, it had not rained since March. Jeff and Darcie were the first to arrive, tools in hand and disappointed to find no one else there. I was so relieved to see them. I had no idea if anyone would come. A half dozen others slowly trickled in, with varying skills and knowledge, willing to help for varying lengths of time. Paul and Maggie, a stylish German couple I had met on one of their many tireless treks around the area, walked up the trail from Finn Bay; Oscar, tall and quiet, arrived wearing his toolbelt; Peter's wife Margaret, soft-spoken and gentle, came with their eleven-month-old baby, Emma, in a sling on her hip. Emma was small and chubby, smiling at everyone.

Slowly it began to take shape. First plastic sheeting was put down, then the floor beams were laid out and hammered into place. I scrambled to make sure they were positioned correctly.

The insulation was placed between the beams, then more plastic was stapled over it for a vapour barrier, and finally the plywood flooring was nailed on top. The ringing tones of several hammers filled the clearing, interspersed with laughter and happy chatter. As the final nails were pounded home, raindrops christened the new floor with unwelcome moisture. It did not seem believable that after so long without rain, it should shower on the day of my house-raising. As the rain grew to a downpour, everyone left. I was dismayed.

An hour later the storm passed and the sun reappeared. Jody and I walked to our quickly drying floor. It stretched out like a large porch in the middle of nowhere, the wall panels stacked hopefully beside it. It was lovely to sit on its smooth warmth surrounded by the trees. The rain had imparted a freshness to the forest, and the birds had begun to sing again. We could hear the rat-tat of a nearby woodpecker and overhead the rasping wings of a raven.

I was feeling disappointed at how little had been done and a bit overwhelmed. The house had not "risen" very high yet. But it was a start.

10. A Doll's House

The weekend was not over yet. My friend from Craig Road, Jeffrey, had not been able to make it to the Saturday house-raising. To my delight, he came Sunday. Jeffrey was fit and healthy, with curly blond hair and light blue, laughing eyes. He had the kind of classical good looks you would expect to find in an artist's depiction of Greek gods. Darcie came to help as well, and together the three of us erected each wall panel and hammered it in place. To my surprise, the level was needed here as well, to make sure each wall stood straight and true.

There had been some confusion over how I was placing the walls. Since I was leaving some of the floor on the outside, I was making the house smaller than it could have been, much to the consternation of those who heard of my plans. They were sure I would later regret this. I didn't waver from my vision of both a firewood porch and an attached greenhouse. Looking back, I suppose that it isn't an orthodox way to create porches by enclosing only part of the floor, but it made sense to me. I wanted the porches much more than a larger house. Luckily, Jeffrey, whose house had given me the idea for the firewood porch, readily accepted my wishes, and Darcie didn't object.

The walls are up

I was fairly used to standing on a ladder by now. My spirits soared as I hammered the boards that tied the walls together, revelling in the strength that had developed in my arms and the house rising below me. It was surprisingly easy and fast, one panel after another until they were all standing tall and firm, braced on each end with a slanted board temporarily nailed into the edge of the wall and the edge of the floor.

Jeffrey demonstrates how to peel a post

What a difference walls made! Now the space was defined. Next I needed to put up the beam that would replace the missing wall. Jeffrey pointed out the logs that could be posts to support this beam. He loaned me his spokeshave, a blade resting between two wooden handles. He demonstrated, propping the log at an angle and sliding the blade smoothly down to strip off the bark. I loved the silky smooth feel of the peeled wood as the log transformed into a post.

The next day I removed the last tenacious remnants of bark and used large spikes to firmly anchor my newly created post in place. I dragged the beam over, wondering how to get it into position. It needed to rest on the top of the two end walls and on the post in the middle of the open space between them. This seemed like an impossibility. I felt so small as my reach came nowhere near those points. I placed a couple of old chairs beside the walls and was able to lift one end of the beam at a time onto them. I could get it no higher. If I tried to lift one end to the top of the wall, the other end would fall. Perhaps if I nailed temporary supports to the ends of the walls I could walk it up there, one step at a time, alternating ends, and climbing on the chairs when needed.

This was exhausting work. My arms ached and sweat trickled down into my eyes. Worse, whenever I got it near the top, I would lose it. The beam would come crashing down and I would have to restart. My frustration climbed higher with every attempt. I felt on the point of tearful collapse, when Dan blundered out of the bush by my house. He was embarrassed, stuttering about misjudging the way, apologizing for being on my property. My spirit soared at this sudden, unexpected potential helper and I halted his hurried departure to explain my dilemma.

"Oh," he sized up the situation.

I held one end as high as I could manage while he placed the other in position. Then we switched. I stood on the chair and kept the beam from slipping, while he lifted the second end into place. Within five minutes it was done and securely nailed. And Dan hurried on his way, my amazed thanks ringing through the forest after him.

I'd had enough for one day. Hot and sweaty, I headed for Jeff and Darcie's to avail myself of their offered bathtub.

The tub sat in their living room, open to view. At some point Darcie would screen it with shower curtains, in deference to the assumed sensibilities of an elderly relative who, in spite of such an effort, did not take a bath the entire week he spent there. At this point however, bathtime was not in the least private. Jody played outside with Terra and Shanti, while Jeff and Darcie alleviated my embarrassment by tactfully averting their eyes. The tub took half an hour to fill with brown-coloured water.

"Country water," Darcie had replied to my hesitant look, vowing its hue was normal for rural water.

Nonetheless it seemed to clean away my grime.

I was out of the tub, dried and just about dressed when their phone rang. Jeff and Darcie had strung phone line hundreds of metres through the bush, laying it carefully across salal and around trees, burying it where it crossed the rough road, all the way to their house. What a feat it seemed to have a phone ring in their off-grid house in the middle of the forest!

"She's here right now, you can ask her yourself," I heard Jeff say. "It's a guy who lives farther up Baggi Road," he remarked as he passed me the phone.

Here was someone I had not met or even heard of. The German-accented voice was that of an older man, gruff and earnest. He had seen my directional signs for the house-raising and wanted to participate. Was there anything left to do?

When I explained the floor was finished and the walls were up, but there was no roof, he replied "My son and I are coming tomorrow to build your roof."

I was speechless. Who was this man?

Heinz was true to his word. The next day he was there with his fifteen-year-old son, Hans, and all his tools. Heinz was a no-nonsense type, gruff, confident, and self-assured. His son was lanky in the way of young teens, dark-eyed and quiet—if he spoke at all, it was in whispers. Heinz quickly let me know that the two of them would do the work by themselves—my role was simply to watch and perhaps answer questions. My offers of help were gently but firmly rebuffed. This was very different from the floor and the walls, when everyone worked together. I couldn't help but think it was the previous generation's view of house construction as a man's job. But I was fine to sit back and let them handle it.

Heinz and Hans working on the roof

Heinz took Jody up on the partially completed roof to hand out the nails and try his hand at hammering a few in. Jody was so pleased. He peeked at me through the rafters, beaming with delight.

I had purchased some rolled roofing, which Heinz explained had to be overlapped more than usual, given that the roof had so little slant. When he and Hans had everything in place, they packed up their tools and left, brushing aside my thanks.

Finishing the roof

A doll's house

The first half of our house was complete. It was open along one side, where I planned to attach the old cabin. As I stood looking at it in the slanting sunlight, it suddenly struck me how much it looked like a metal doll's house I'd had as a child. I remembered one long wall had been missing, so my little hand could reach in to all the rooms. It was a comforting thought that we would be living in a house almost like the doll's house I had so enjoyed playing with many years before.

The next day I carefully replaced the missing window that had been removed during construction. It looked out over the wood porch I insisted on leaving outside. The window, though not down at floor level like Jeffrey's, would be the "wood window" through which firewood could be reached. I nailed the original front steps halfway along the open side. Then I staple-gunned blankets along the edge of the ceiling beam, the floor, and the walls to keep out mosquitoes. In the freezing cold of the previous winter, Darcie gave us an extra long dark brown blanket. She told me the story of how chilly their house had been their first winter in Lund. A relative visited during this cold time and, although now their finished place was well-heated, he continued to gift them warm blankets every year.

I was so grateful to her for this lovely soft warmth during our shivery winter nights. And now I was delighted to have a blanket long enough to serve as our door. I attached it only along the ceiling in the middle of the beam so it could be pushed open to enter and exit, but would fall back into place and prevent bugs from invading our space. The opening to the projected greenhouse was covered the same way. Now our house was snug and cozy.

When Darcie dropped by, I was proud to show her how I had closed off the open side, but she wasn't pleased. She surprised me by objecting to the use of her blanket as my door and asked me pointedly to take it down. She thought it would get dirty and possibly ripped, and insisted she had only loaned it to me for use as bedding. Oh dear! I was unaware that she wanted it back eventually; I mistakenly thought she had given it to me. I felt very bad when she left, but it made such a perfect door and I could think of nothing I could use to replace it. I worried about it for days, mulling over what I might do. In the end, I guiltily decided to leave it where it was until I could finish closing in the house. I hoped I could make sure the lovely blanket was never damaged and I planned to clean and return it as soon as I could take it down. I was nervous about Darcie coming over and seeing it still stapled up. When she did finally pay another visit, to my great relief, she didn't mention it. Did I dare hope she had forgotten about it?

In fact, it wasn't spoken of until I brought it over to her place months later, newly dry-cleaned and beautifully folded inside the cleaner's plastic bag. I was glad to show her it was still in perfect condition and explain why I hadn't done as she asked. She confessed that she had hidden her upset at my non-compliance because she hadn't known what to say. Now she was embarrassed that I had gone to the trouble of dry-cleaning it and was relieved to see it was in fine shape. It was so good to clear the air between us, to have both of our feelings and unsaid words heard and accepted.

But all of that would come later. Right now, it was July again; one year had passed since our arrival in Lund. And we were ready to move in.

11. Secret Treasures

Fitting all our belongings into the little half-house proved impossible. I drew the floor plan and cut to scale paper representations of our meagre furniture, so I could play with fitting them all into the less than 200 square foot room.

The counter could stand unattached under the only window, a bucket of water and a dishpan gracing its top, beside our small stack of dishes. We kept our perishables in the old cooler tucked under the house and our dry food in the van, parked in the shade and closed up tight against rodents and insects. The tiny propane stove from the van continued to cook our food. I served it on the wooden table long abandoned in the old cabin, and we sat together on a couple of mismatched chairs similarly left behind. Some of our belongings were packed into boxes and stored in our old canvas tent, which I set up nearby, not for a moment considering that unheated canvas would be no match for coastal dampness.

Jody's brightly painted desk stood cheerfully at the foot of his small bed, which was tucked into the darkest corner, snugged up against the blanket wall. Directly across, my mattress ran along the rear wall, the head against the grey blanket that hung over the opening to the future greenhouse.

Breezes would blow this blanket past my head and I would wake to see the countless immensity of stars above me. One very early morning, I peeked under it to watch a black bear snuffling and munching berries not twenty feet from where I lay. His glossy coat shone in the early morning light as he ambled, unaware of my breathless scrutiny. I felt privileged and vulnerable. I wanted to share the wonder of it with Jody, still asleep in his own bed, but dared not make the slightest sound. I watched the large animal out of sight, then lay smiling to myself, amazed at what I had seen.

Now that we were living up Steller Road, the old wishing well was too far away to haul our water. For five dollars I bought a large plastic rain barrel. It fit in the back of the van, but I was unsure where I could get water to fill it. Neil informed me that there was a water hose on the Lund dock. It was probably for boaters to use. I brazenly drove out on the dock and filled the fifty-five gallon barrel as full as I dared. I was a little nervous, but no one said anything to me. My van took the weight without complaint and I drove slowly back through the potholes and over the hills. Now I felt rich with water. I had no way to remove the heavy barrel from the van, but I could scoop it into my five gallon container, which had a spigot. It sat on the counter, merrily dispensing water and I refilled it from the barrel whenever it ran low. It was always nerve-wracking to drive back onto the Lund dock to use that hose again; luckily it was a long time between barrel replenishments.

The open well we previously used had long been a worry to me. I approached Dan, whose land it sat on. Dan didn't actually own the land; he was only squatting there, though he had put a lot of work into it and made amazing improvements to it. He had no idea who had dug the well and, though he was fine with my filling it in, didn't want to take responsibility for financing such a remedy. He suggested I find someone who would do it and determine the cost, then approach everyone who lived nearby and ask them to split the price, since it would be for the benefit of the whole neighbourhood.

Since many of the neighbours complained to me of the danger and affirmed that it "ought to be filled in," I was optimistic about the outcome of canvassing them. However, while I suppose it was easy to state something really should be done, committing to pay for it was more challenging. Right away I sensed a reluctance. A common reaction was "if everyone else agrees," they would unenthusiastically go along. Since no one gave me an outright "No," I plowed ahead, telling each that everyone else had agreed and collecting their share of the price. Dan was only too happy to pay a share as well.

The day it was filled in was an exciting one. Jody and I went down to watch. The huge dump truck backed up to the well and dumped a tremendous amount of gravel in, dust and water spraying everywhere. Then we waited while he went back for another load of gravel. In the end, it took almost three loads. When the deep hole was finally gone and a small rounded bump of gravel rose in its place, Jody and I stood on top of it, triumphant and safe.

The neighbours, however, were less than pleased. They felt that no one had truly agreed to it. They challenged my process, suggesting a meeting should have been held to discuss it. Many of them thought Dan should have been responsible for the cost, or me, since I had been the one worried about it. I was sorry for any bad feelings, but it was too late now. The money had been collected and spent, and the well was no more.

Our part-house, part-tent was fine in the heat of summer, but I knew we would need four solid walls before autumn crept onto our doorstep. The old cabin would be the second house I dismantled, but if I felt experienced and knowledgeable in the art of demolition, I was in for a rude awakening. To take down a recently built pre-fab house, made to come apart in panels, in no way prepared me for the arduous task of removing a permanent cabin that had aged and settled over the course of decades, its nails rusting in place and its recesses hiding insect damage and rot.

I was glad I had tackled the easier house first. The nails in this cabin were very difficult to extract, and I sweated and put my whole weight into prying some of them out. Often the head of the nail would break off, or its edges fold flat, making it impossible for my trusty cat's claw to grasp. Some boards would break when I tried to remove them. Everything was full of the accumulated dust and dirt of years.

Each board had to be labelled and transcribed onto a diagram that showed where it would be installed in our new house. Because I had very little knowledge of how to build a house, I had to copy what had previously been done. I had absolute faith and trust in the unknown people who had constructed this cabin so long ago. Whatever boards and supports they used, I was forced to repeat, not knowing enough to change or try to improve upon what they had done. Those that were not reusable would have to be replaced; that too was noted on the diagram.

Once, as I made my way down to work on the old cabin, I stepped onto the road at the bottom of the hill and startled a large black bear about halfway up. He faced me and rose up on his hind legs. I froze, wondering what I should do. We stared at each other for what seemed several minutes. I took in how big he was, so much taller and heavier than I. And yet there was no menace in his look. He seemed more unsure than threatening. Then in a fluid motion, he dropped to all fours and slipped into the trees. I could hear the crashing of his progress quickly receding. I let out the breath I hadn't realized I'd been holding and shakily walked up the hill past the spot where he had stood. I was laughing softly with relief and the wonder of it all.

The old cabin was much more exposed than the pre-fab had been. Instead of a secluded clearing, I now worked right beside the road. True, this was not a very frequented road, but there was no guarantee that someone wouldn't pass by, as I found to my embarrassment one hot afternoon when I laboured topless up on the open floor of the loft. I kept my back turned and prayed that Dan would stop asking questions and take the hint to move on. As soon as he was out of sight, I hurriedly replaced my shirt, prepared to put up with the heat, which in any case seemed less than the heat radiating from my blushing face.

Another time when Dan was passing by, he stopped to ask if I knew the day. He wasn't sure if it was Monday or Tuesday. I looked at him, agape.

"Today's Thursday," I said.

He didn't believe me at first. "No, it can't be."

But I knew for certain it was, because I had been to town just the day before for a Wednesday appointment.

When I finally convinced him, he walked down the hill muttering to himself, "Two days! How could I have lost two days?"

I chuckled softly, thinking of how far removed Jody and I were now from tightly scheduled city lives.

The loft flooring contained a maze of tunnels where the carpenter ants had lived. I held my breath when I pried them up with shaking hands, but to my great relief, not a single ant remained. There were more tunnels than wood in those boards. It was a scary thought that we had been walking on such a thin shell.

As I took the cabin slowly apart, piece by piece, I wondered about the people who had built it so long before, and those who had lived there in the ensuing years. Had they loved it or wanted out? Would they be sad to see it come down, or glad that it would live again as part of our house? I could not hear the laughter or the tears it had previously contained, but the cabin had secrets to share with me.

As I took apart the loft flooring, an old photo fell to the floor below. A sepia print on stained cardboard, it was a beautiful picture of an infant cupid with colourized cheeks. I fell in love with its charm and its mystery. With trepidation I asked everyone I knew who had a connection to the old cabin, but no one could tell me anything about it. I was free to keep it and it has always been one of my treasured possessions.

The old photo

The windows in the old cabin were ancient, with wooden frames and peeling paint. They were lovingly put aside. I smiled when I thought of the character they would add to our new house.

The purple spires of lupine had long been a favourite of mine. I had picked a seed pod the previous fall and placed it on the downstairs windowsill. I hoped to scatter the seeds near our house site, but the pod had burst and the seeds vanished. As I took apart the wall under the window and the flooring nearby, I kept an eye out for the errant seeds. I did not find them, but a greater treasure awaited me.

The silver chain was fine and fragile looking, the long pendant tarnished. I stared at the velvety blue oval gemstone. I had never seen anything like it. When sunlight struck it, the white rays of a star crossed its face; they vanished when I held it in the shade. I owned no real jewellery and this beautiful necklace looked very valuable to me. Surely its owner must be missing it. Had it dropped unnoticed into the floorboards, leaving the owner fruitlessly searching in all the wrong places? Or had they seen its sudden unanticipated exit and tried in vain to follow with knife-edge and tweezers? Such regal beauty to be trapped in the rough floor boards of a poor cabin. Several people informed me that it was a star sapphire, but no one could be found to claim it. To this day, it remains a precious souvenir of my work that summer.

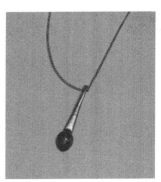

Star sapphire necklace

Finally the old cabin was no more. It lay in pieces that were easily loaded into my van and transported up to our half-house.

And the following spring, lupines bloomed where that

cabin had once stood. I dug them up carefully and replanted them outside our new front door.

The transplanted lupines

12. Two Halves Make a Whole

When I stood in my little half-house and slowly turned in a circle, I could picture the living room it would become. Sighing, I turned my attention to the missing half, the part I now needed to construct: a warm, cozy kitchen, with our sleeping loft above it. I built the floor by myself this time, confidently wielding the level and smiling at the ease with which the beams lined up, level and true, one after the other. The two halves became one when I triumphantly nailed together the two floor beams along the open edge. To my pleased surprise, the plywood flooring abutted with barely a crack.

"Look," I called to Jody, "the new floor is like a giant porch."

His smile matched mine as he ran to get some toys. It was a wonderful surface for his cars to drive on and his Playmobil figures to act out their elaborate games.

I carried Jody's desk out there and set up his blue Raggedy Ann and Andy child-size table and its folding chairs. His excitement was contagious and I put my building plans briefly on hold to hang homemade swings and knotted blue ropes from the beam. From a tree on the other side of the house dangled our old monkey swing, a sturdy red plastic circle Jody had enjoyed in Victoria. The rope passed through its centre, and Jody could balance sitting on it, swaying and turning in circles, or swing hanging from the handgrips underneath. In the weeks that followed he tried out ever more difficult acrobatics while I worked on the house, occasionally pausing to watch his fun. The summer continued as it had begun: sunny and warm. We usually carried our food out to our temporary porch, and ate under the blue sky and waving green branches.

The bright orange flash of flickers fluttering overhead was a common sight. I had long been mystified hearing the piercing call of what sounded to me like a jungle bird high in the trees. Now we enjoyed these magnificent large flyers as they frequented the arbutus trees that surrounded our house, drumming like woodpeckers, searching on the ground for insects, or feasting on the treetop berries. Finding one of the striking orange feathers dropped from a flicker's wing was a delight.

There were many distractions from house-building. The warm sunshine beckoned me to put down my tools and enjoy the summertime. Jody began swimming lessons in town, and I signed him up for a gym program too. There was a Lund Summer Day Camp he participated in, doing crafts and playing games with others his age. He attended organized activities at the Powell River Recreation Complex as well: Exploring the Seashore, Coastal Plant Life, and one called Nature Knowledge. Jody went to them all, excited and exuberant when each event came up. There was Willybugs at the beach one afternoon, an Outdoor Pool Fun Meet one morning, and a picnic at Palm Beach, south of town. Jody glowed through the summer.

In between all the fun activities, I doggedly continued on. The three remaining panels from Doug's pre-fab could simply be stood up and hammered into place. As I attempted to do this, I was distraught to discover that a large fir tree grew too close to what would be the south wall of the kitchen. What to do? It seemed so unfair that a tree which had grown strong and tall for hundreds of years had to come down just because I had decided to build our house there. There seemed to be no other choice. I wrapped my arms around the doomed tree in a heartfelt hug, murmuring my regrets, before biting my lip and firing up the chainsaw.

I attached the two panels with windows to form the kitchen's south wall, so that whether I stood at the counter or sat at the table, I could watch the world and the weather outside. The final panel held our only door. It was a grey aluminum screen door and, with help, I hammered it at the end of an entryway that I planned to line with hooks for our coats and with shelves for cool storage. The neighbours ridiculed me for calling this a vestibule.

"Around here," Jeff smiled, "we call it a mud room."

Such an ugly name! I knew I would never call it that. In the end, we came to refer to it simply as "the pantry."

Yvon came by to help on the house from time to time and to spend the night. He intrigued me with tales of something called "rebirthing." I wasn't sure what was involved, but Yvon had done it several times and it had powerfully affected him. He strongly recommended I try it, and curious, I agreed.

A large number of us gathered in a big empty room, laying on sleeping bags we had each brought. Rebirthing involves an extended period of circular breathing, where each breath in and out is followed by another without the slightest pause. We were warned about possible symptoms: tingling, numbness, blacking out.

"Hmm," I thought skeptically, "it sounds like hyperventilating to me."

Supposedly we might relive our birth. It was hard for me to relax; I couldn't keep my eyes closed without draping my arm over them. No one else seemed to have this problem. I was surprised Yvon loved this boring activity so much. After an interminable time, I became aware of people talking. Some were crying, some whispering. I opened my eyes, conscious of how cold I was. Freezing, though the temperature of the room was very high. Someone came over to debrief me, and then went to fetch blankets. And more blankets, even sleeping bags. It didn't matter how many they piled on me, I was still cold. Was this what I had felt at my birth? Or was it just a result of hyperventilating? Yvon was disappointed in my lack of enthusiasm and suggested I try it again. But rebirthing was not something I ever wanted to do a second time. Just one other area where Yvon and I didn't concur. It had given me a brief break from the constant work of building the house, but I was anxious to get back to it.

With the last panel in place, I knew the easy part was behind me. The rest of the walls had to be rebuilt from the parts of the old cabin, piece by piece, like fitting a giant three-dimensional jigsaw puzzle back together. It was painstakingly slow working on this by myself. To my delight, friends, acquaintances, and even strangers occasionally dropped in on me to lend a hand. I wasn't sure who these men were or how they had found me hidden away so far from the main roads. And where were the women?

I didn't spend a lot of time wondering why there was suddenly a man or two hanging around. I thought perhaps men were more interested and knowledgeable about house construction. Naively, it never occurred to me that they might have romantic hopes. I simply accepted their help without question, delighted to be able to tap their knowledge and rely on their strength. I supposed that I must have been something of a curiosity and was more concerned with getting my questions answered and quickening the pace as the weeks rolled by towards autumn. The nights turned cooler and plywood replaced the hanging blanket by the head of my bed, which meant we could no longer duck under it to sit on the tiny floor of the hoped for greenhouse. Wild geese could be heard over the sound of hammering, calling a warning as they fled south.

The borrowed woodstove I used the previous winter had been reclaimed by Sean. I searched out the perfect cast-iron stove, and found what I was looking for in an ad in one of my homesteading magazines. The Consolidated Dutchwest model had glass doors in the front, a cooking square on top, and grating that could be turned to dump ashes into a drawer for emptying. There was a brass rod on the side for hanging mittens or socks to dry. It had a catalytic converter for efficient burning and even a thermometer for monitoring the fire's level. It would be not only the most expensive item in my house, but likely cost more than the house itself. The only problem was that the American company would not deliver it to Lund, or even to Powell River. I had to drive to Vancouver to collect it. I hoped my old Ford Econoline van was up to the task. With excitement and some trepidation, I reluctantly left behind my work-in-progress and, with Jody, headed down the coast to the big city.

Once arrived, I backed up to the warehouse loading dock and held my breath while the forklift picked up the crated stove and placed it in the back of my van. Driving home was easy, but I had no idea how to get it out of my van, never mind up and over the thirty feet of rocks to get it into the house. Dan assured me half a dozen strong men should be able to carry it. The problem was how to get that many up to my house at the same time. Somehow it all came together. First, the stove had to be detached from the pallet. The men then insisted on ripping off the cardboard box, which I had wanted to save for Jody to play in. There seemed no way around it, so I finally, reluctantly agreed. With great difficulty they lowered it from the van, amazed by how heavy it was. One of them had the clever idea to remove the doors and it was discovered that it contained many loose heavy parts, like the shaker grates, that could be taken out to lessen the load. And in the end the stove was in the house and the men left with much back-slapping and hearty congratulations among them, and many thank-yous and hugs from me.

They weren't able to place the stove exactly where it needed to be because I first had to gather the bricks to rest it on. Alone I wiggled my shiny stove into place beneath the hole in the roof, which was as near to the centre of the house as I could manage. I struggled to lift one leg at a time onto a brick, and then filled in the rest of the bricks underneath, so it sat safely on a fireproof layer. I purchased an insulated stovepipe to go through the roof. The stovepipe pointed arrow straight, reaching safely up past the highest point of the soon to be completed barn-shaped roof. I proudly stood back, satisfied that the coming winter cold could be kept at bay.

With the stove in place, I could turn my attention to the upstairs. I happily carried the beams for the loft floor up the ladder one at a time, and placed them on the roof of the completed first half of my house, above where the living room would be. I was delighted to have such a work surface, better than any scaffolding. It seemed amazing that the house had come so far. I loved working up at this level, up in the trees really, the birds fluttering around me. I had been disappointed to learn that there was no possibility of a view to the ocean. If I crossed the border of the tenancy in common lands, I could see the water and Savary Island, with the mountains of Vancouver Island behind. It was exasperating to have an ocean view from so near and yet not from our piece. Jody and I would often walk to a rocky ridge just over the border of our land to admire the view and have a picnic. If we were lucky, we might catch a glimpse of an alligator lizard who sunned himself among the rocks, disappearing in a blur if disturbed. Working up on top of the house, if I looked to the south through the thick branches and the straight trunks, I could see bright sparkling light. When Heinz was working on the living room roof, he had asked if I knew that was sunlight shining on the water.

"I bet you'd have a view of the ocean if you took down about half a dozen trees."

Really? That would be very strange, an impossibly fortuitous chance that had me choose the one house site that held a possibility of the view I had long ago given up on.

Once all the loft beams had been carried up there, I began attaching them to the top of the walls, one step above the living room roof. While nailing down the loft floorboards, the ache in my right wrist, which had been slowly worsening, became unbearable. This frightened me because there was still much hammering left to do. A trip to a doctor in town had me diagnosed with tenosynovitis. A bubblegum pink plastic brace was molded to fit my child-size wrist and forearm. I had no intention of following the doctor's orders to stop hammering—that was not an option. Every morning I faithfully strapped on the brace, hating the queasy-looking colour, and carried on. New boards replaced the old ant-tunnelled loft flooring and the heavy wooden ladder rose once again to connect the two floors. This time I firmly nailed it in place.

The roof above the loft was a daunting project. I rebuilt the barn-shaped rafters, each one made of four pieces on which I had traced the angles I needed to recreate. I managed, fearfully and with great difficulty, to raise one into place, towering high above my head. How I wished once again that my reach extended higher. The first rafter was the hardest; I came close to losing it over the edge as I struggled to keep the weight of it upright and nail it at the same time. When it was firmly attached, I had to sit in the sunshine next to it and wait for my thumping heart to slow and my breathing to normalize. I steeled myself for the next, but the others weren't as nerve-wracking. I still had to work hard to keep them upright while attaching them, but at least they weren't teetering on the edge. I laid each one out in position on the loft flooring, then slowly raised it upright. One after another they marched along, until there was no longer the room to lay out the next. I was stumped. I couldn't figure out how to erect the remaining few, and especially the one on the other edge. I knew I needed help.

Barn-shaped rafters up

Asking for advice elicited a flurry of friends to my aid, mystified as to how I had managed to erect them alone. Explaining my process only had them shaking their heads. With extra hands it was easy; we could simply stand them up on the living room roof and carry them into place. After they were all up, the next step defeated me. I knew they needed to be joined together at the highest point by a long board, called a ridgepole. The rafters loomed way above me, far out of reach, even from the top of the ladder. My helpers were fearful, even horrified, that I might try to do it by myself, and once again came to my aid. Once the ridgepole was in place, the roof and the loft's end walls would need to be covered in plywood. And then finally, the roof would need cedar shakes to fend off the rain.

The old cabin's roof had only been half covered in shakes, and none of them had survived the demolition. A number of huge cedar rounds had decorated the area around the old cabin. Jody enjoyed playing on these, a surface for his toys, and sometimes he even climbed up to stand on top of them. Don transported these rounds up to my house site and found others abandoned in the forest to add to them. I planned to turn them into cedar shakes. Jeffrey loaned me his froe, a long wedge-shaped tool with a handle. He showed me how to place the froe, bang it into the round with a mallet, then pull the handle towards me. Pop! A perfect shake would snap free of the round and fall to the ground. It was easy and fun and almost like magic. Every day I made a few more shakes and steadfastly piled them up beside the unfinished house. I used the easy rounds first. Those that had branches were much more difficult, requiring more force to snap out the shake. As I got down to the harder, branchier bolts, the froe had to be followed by wedges driving it deeper into the bolt. How many shakes would I need? It seemed an endless number and the task lost its element of fun, becoming an arduous chore I longed to be finished.

When I had enough to cover half the roof, I took a break. It would be a long break. The half that could be reached from the living room roof would be easy to shake. I could do that later, I reasoned. In fact, winter descended before I could turn my attention to shaking that half. It would remain in plastic-covered plywood for the next couple of years.

The far side of the roof took priority for the shakes I had

made. First it would need plywood. It was so very high, with rock below. I trembled at even the thought of going up that far. How could I ever work on such a steep roof? Once again I would need help. I asked anyone who came by, until finally I was given the name of a fellow I might be able to hire to complete this task. Mike agreed, though not without trepidation. He swallowed audibly before ascending. I held the ladder, but strongly doubted I would be able to support him if it began to fall. I said nothing. My hope and fear combined in a lump at the base of my throat. I tried to call cheerfully up, shading my eyes and squinting to watch his progress. I also helped support each piece of plywood as Mike struggled to bring it up the ladder. When the roof was at last covered in plywood, I had to find someone else who would install the shakes I had laboured so hard to make.

In the meantime, the number of felled cedar trees I had left lying around the garden area gave me an idea. I had found a do-it-yourself book at the library on how to make playground equipment out of logs. I was expert at peeling them now. Studying carefully the diagrams and instructions, I drilled holes through the logs and attached them together with huge bolts. I built a square of logs, topped by slightly smaller squares, forming steps to climb on all sides. Jody tried it out, climbing it every time I added another set of logs. After three sets, I topped it with a platform made of logs bolted side by side. It was a fantastic play structure! Thrilled, I proceeded to build two more such structures even higher, that I connected with a wide, strong board as a bridge between them. Somewhere we found an old steering wheel and I hammered it into place on the arbutus that grew in the shape of a bench, where we first sat to eat our lunch. Now it was a pretend car for Jody to drive.

Another summer was ending, but this year we discovered a fun way to mark its passage: the Sunshine Coast Folkfest. Every Labour Day weekend, an amazing music festival is held at Palm Beach, south of Powell River. It's an idyllic location: the grassy park leads onto stretches of warm sand and climbable rocks bordering a protected bay. Sailboats moor off shore, and swimmers brave the cool waters, while melodies and harmonies drift across the waves. Local artisans hawk their crafty wares and enticing smells waft from the food stalls. If you don't like the music, just wait: a different singer or band will be on every half hour or so.

In 1985, Labour Day weekend, and therefore the Folkfest, began on the last day of August. That was the day I brought Jody to what would become our yearly end-of-the-summer tradition. It wasn't expensive, less than ten dollars I think, and Jody was free. We spread out our blanket under an enormous open-sided tent and sat cross-legged amidst almost all the friends and acquaintances I'd met during my year in Lund. I sat with Yvon, though our relationship was in its final stages. We were drifting apart and rarely saw each other now. It was a cloudless, warm day and I felt suspended in time, immersed in the ever-changing, beautiful music.

Greg, who I had first met at the Healing Gathering and gotten to know better when we both stayed on afterward at Jeffrey's, had an invitation for us. He was a big guy and he shouted to be heard over the blaring speakers of one of the louder musical groups. Greg wanted to invite us to a family-friendly party that night at the house he shared with his girlfriend, Mary, not far from Palm Beach. We decided to go.

The party was full of many that I knew and many that I didn't. Yvon and Jody found a huge book about machines and passed almost the whole party seated at a table excitedly discussing each picture. I drifted from room to room, till I saw a curly-haired fellow playing guitar and singing. I have always found such serenading attractive and romantic. He seemed at ease, joking and smiling as he sang the sweet old-fashioned love songs. I joined the small group sitting around him, listening or making requests. When he took a break, he chatted with us, his audience. I mentioned that I hadn't seen him at the Folkfest, and he explained that he hadn't been there, deeming it too expensive in his unemployed state. I learned he was a friend of Mary's and recently arrived from Winnipeg. His name was Barry. Intrigued, I hoped I might run into him again.

It was at the party that I found out Mary and Greg were opening a café at the corner of Marine and Joyce in Powell River, which they named *R Place*. This became a favourite stop for Jody and me to recoup in the middle of a busy town day or just to pass the time while waiting for an appointment or one of Jody's scheduled activities. Mary suggested I could help out by cleaning the bathrooms, sweeping the floors, or emptying the trash, and she would pay me in muffins or other goodies. It was a great arrangement, and I looked forward to visiting with them whenever we headed into town.

It was there that I met again, and really got to know, Barry, who was working for muffins, just like me. We teamed up on certain jobs and sat together chatting while munching our earnings. When I suggested he visit me out in Lund, he asked me to draw him a map, which I sketched out on a napkin. I freely invited everyone I met to come visit, but no one had taken me up on it, perhaps hesitant to travel so far out of the way or to brave the twisty, rutted maze of back roads beyond the village of Lund. I certainly didn't expect Barry to actually arrive at my cabin, nor did I imagine, in my wildest dreams, the romance and magic and the long-awaited answer to my deepest hopes that were lurking just ahead.

After the Folkfest, I coated the plywood floor of my almost-finished house with paint from a partially used can I had come across somewhere. I left an unpainted path to walk on, then the following day finished that part, stepping on newspapers laid down to show where the floor was already dry. The old paint can had optimistically assured us it would be a lovely, muted shade of brown, but the dry floor looked distinctly purplish. Oh well. It was all done and dried just in time for Jody to celebrate his eighth birthday, with his lively friends cavorting over the spotless floor and spilling out into the forest. Bright coloured party hats gleamed in the sunshine among the trees decked with balloons, which popped in a startling way when a slight breeze blew them onto prickly twigs. I had finally found someone that I could hire to attach the shakes on the steep part of the roof. Steve grinned to see the party guests at their fun. When it ended and all had been bundled off home, I left Jody to play with his new toys and stood at the bottom of the ladder, handing up the shakes. One by one he nailed them in place, and I delighted to see them slowly covering that high, dangerous side. I was so proud of having made all the shakes by hand.

And then suddenly, to my amazement, our house was complete. It seemed unbelievable! With the help of so many wonderful friends and neighbours, whose priceless advice had more than made up for my woeful lack of construction knowledge, we had finished the house, and barely in time. It was early October and frost already surprised our early mornings. Steller Place was as yet uninsulated and had no interior walls. None of that mattered. I could continue puttering away at it from inside while living in it. The dream I had set out to accomplish, the dream that had seemed so impossible and had met so many obstacles, had been achieved. I had bought my land and built my house. Tears sprung to my eyes as I stood surveying the little three-room cabin that had taken so much work and effort, luck and love. Hand in hand, Jody and I walked inside, closing the door behind us.

Terry Faubert

Epilogue: Five Years Later

Jody, me, Kyle   Robin

The sun streams in the kitchen window as I stand at the sink. Dark, curly-haired Robin, almost four, plays with his cars at my feet; Kyle, blue-eyed and blond, my youngest son, sits on my hip in the sling, smiling at the bubbles as I wash another bowl. I love to work here where a casual glance to the left shows me what I had longed to see: those trees finally did come down to give us our beautiful view. Sailboats skitter through the waves, cruise ships float majestically by, and the sandy shores of Savary Island beckon. The snow-capped mountains of far-off Vancouver Island soar upward to form the impressive horizon. Jody, just turned thirteen, dashes in at breakneck speed, followed by our unstoppable blonde cocker spaniel, Max, his long silky ears flapping with each joyful bound.

Jody and Max

The outside of our house is now painted dark brown. Our solid grey brick chimney stretches above the solar panels that grace our roof. A government grant paid for our drilled well, our generator, and plumbing to the house. Propane cooks our food, heats our water, runs our fridge, and dries Kyle's cloth diapers. We went from using candles to kerosene lanterns, to propane lights, and finally now twelve-volt electric lights chase away the dark nights. The house has power from three separate sources: the generator for power-hungry appliances like the washing machine and the vacuum cleaner, the twelve-volt system directly from our huge battery bank via the solar panels, and an inverter that changes the twelve-volt to house current.

Yes, my little cabin can now truly be called a house. My tall, young husband, Barry, has wild, curly dark hair, a full reddish beard, and the lightest blue eyes I've ever seen. The first time he visited, he helped me insulate the bare walls, while his young dog Max ran barking around the house with Jody. Barry offered to replace the old loft ladder with stairs and went on to expand and extend the building, attaching additions and transforming the little cabin into a real house. The loft became a full second storey and a room was added even above that. I never did get the attached greenhouse of my dreams, though a plastic-covered greenhouse stands proudly beside the garden. The unfinished end of the living room was absorbed into the house complete with two giant windows. We always refer to it as "the extension."

Barry

Jody heads upstairs to work on his MS-DOS laptop computer, organizing his neighbourhood detective club, making games for his little brother, printing posters, and writing stories. It won't be long until he leaves behind his childhood name, maturing into Joseph.

Most of our fruit and vegetables come from our garden. The layered method I learned from Kurt, coupled with the rich bog soil I carted by hand, produces a plentiful supply of everything from corn to raspberries. Our Northern Spy tree grows the best-tasting apples ever, in abundance. We gather eggs from our brown chickens, scratching and clucking near the house and from our white ducks, gracefully paddling around the pond we had dug out. Soon we will add goats to our menagerie, along with rabbits and even pigeons. Furry's descendants maintain an uneasy peace with Max, tracking his erratic movements from high places.

Life in the bush isn't always easy: starting the generator, filling the propane tanks, pumping the water, getting in the firewood, all take much time and major effort. Yet my heart sings as I gaze out the window. Trees embrace the house on every side. At night stars twinkle through their branches and the dazzling Milky Way spreads across the darkness.

The moon casts shadows on clear nights and bats flit through them. My days are filled with the laughter of children, running free with the wind at their heels, climbing trees, hiding in the hollows under boulders, building tree houses.

For over seventeen years, we will live here, past the turn of the century, till Joseph has grown up and left home and Robin is a teenager, Kyle an eleven-year-old. By then, my wonderful daughter, Laura, will have completed our family, her blond curls bouncing as she scampers among the trees with her brothers. And less than two years after her arrival, while we're still living here, Barry will leave us to seek other adventures.

I cannot see this future as I stand at the sink that sunny day, content to be living in the forest, where even mundane tasks like washing dishes hold beauty. I marvel to be here. It *is* like camping forever. My children *are* growing up wise to the ways of nature. And Cristel was right: it was indeed out in the country that I found my country guy to love. What an amazing adventure—the greatest adventure of my life—this turned out to be!

Terry Faubert

Photo Credits

Most of the photos in this book are the property of the author. The exceptions are noted here, with thanks for the photographer's permission to use them.

Pg 10, D. McLean

Pg 30, Mary Good, (Peter and Linda's farm)

Pg 30, bottom, Y. Ricard

Pg 31, Y. Ricard

Pg 44, D. McLean

Pg 45, D. McLean, (We arrive!)

Pg 46, D. McLean

Pg 49, D. McLean

Pg 92, D. McLean

Pg 139, Rolland Desilets, (Robin)

Pg 149, Rick Turcotte

Back Cover, D. McLean

Terry Faubert

Acknowledgements

I owe an enormous debt of gratitude to Sandra Tonn. She is an amazing memoir teacher and mentor. She can take a group of seniors who have never penned their memories and, in a few short weeks, transform them all into fine writers. Without her knowledge, support, and constructive critiques, this book would never have been written. Her feedback, on both the initial draft and the final product, has been crucial to my shaping of this story.

I also wish to thank the members of my monthly memoir writing group: Joanna Dunbar, Vi Issac, Mary Lou MacMillan, Lynn McCann, Rita Rasmussen, Teresa Rice, George Samuel, and Rose Marie Williams. Month by month, chapter by chapter, their suggestions and encouragement helped me hone in on what was important and identify what was missing. You have no idea how much that helped me.

I would like to acknowledge four gracious people who agreed to read over my manuscript and provide feedback: Winnie Ferrier, Diane Fraser, Carol Jones, and especially Margy Lutz for her astute comments and grammar corrections. The suggestions and ideas you all expressed were extremely valuable. And I can't forget Christy Ziegler, who did a superb job of copy-editing the final manuscript. I'd also like to thank Joanna Dunbar for her helpful advice on the cover and Katie McLean for her crucial assistance with its formatting.

Last of all, I wish to thank again Jeff and Darcie MacFronton and all the rest of my wonderful friends and neighbours in Lund, whose advice, skills, strength, and tools helped bring my hoped-for house to fruition. I could not have done it without each and every one of you.

Terry Faubert

About the Author

Terry Faubert was born in the early 1950s in Toronto, Ontario. She moved to Canada's west coast in 1978. All of her working life was spent in the field of early childhood education: in day care, preschool, and supported child development.

An avid hiker, she has walked hundreds of kilometres on Canada's Great Trail in British Columbia, the Camino de Santiago in northern Spain, the Sunshine Coast Trail near Powell River, and numerous others.

Terry has had short stories published in four memoir anthologies: *Slices* (2013), *Taboo* (2016), *Turning Points* (2018), *Tricky* (2018) and in three issues of the *Lund Barnacle* (Fall 2017, Winter 2018, Spring 2018).

She has four grown children and two grandchildren. She currently resides in Powell River B.C. with her tortoiseshell cat, Briar. This is her first book-length memoir.

Made in the USA
Columbia, SC
16 October 2021